نواب شجاع الدوله بهادر

LUCKNOW
City of Illusion

Edited by

Rosie Llewellyn-Jones

With a Preface by

E. Alkazi

Contributions by

Rosie Llewellyn-Jones, Peter Chelkowski, Neeta Das,
Nina David, Sophie Gordon, and Stéphanie Roy

The Alkazi Collection of Photography
New York · London · New Delhi

Prestel
Munich · Berlin · London · New York

This book has been designed by E. Alkazi.

© for text and images: The Alkazi Collection of Photography, 2006
with the exception of the illustrations listed below.
© for layout and production: Prestel Verlag
Munich · Berlin · London · New York 2006

Published by Prestel in association
with The Alkazi Collection of Photography.

The rights of E. Alkazi, Rosie Llewellyn-Jones, Peter Chelkowski,
Neeta Das, Nina David, Sophie Gordon and Stéphanie Roy
to be identified as authors of this work have been asserted in accordance
with the Copyright, Designs and Patents Act 1988.

Photo Credits:
© Tate, London 2003 (fig. 2)
Collection Centre Canadien d'Architecture/Canadian Centre
for Architecture, Montreal (figs. 105, 128)
© Christie's Images Ltd. 2004 (fig. 33)
By permission of the British Library (figs. 3, 9, 10, 12, 13, 14, 93, 94,
104, 107, 116, 133, List of Nawabs: Ghazi-ud-din Haider)
V&A Picture Library (frontispiece; figs. 6, 7, 18)
By permission of the Trustees of the Victoria Memorial, Kolkata (fig. 131)
La Martinière College, Lucknow (fig. 135)
Private Collection, London (figs. 16, 19)
W. Sypniewski (figs. 52, 53, 62, 63, 64, 65, 66)
R. Llewellyn-Jones (figs. 91, 140, 141, 142)
N. Das (fig. 108)

Cover: Clifton & Co., *Asafi Mosque and Bara Imambara
viewed from the Rumi Darwaza*, c. 1900.
Frontispiece: Mihr Chand after Tilly Kettle, *Portrait of Shuja-ud-daula
in Tartar Dress*, oil painting, Faizabad, c. 1772.
Front endpapers: Frith's Series, *Chaulakhi Gateway, leading out
of the Jilau Khana, Qaisarbagh*, albumen print, mid-1870s.
Back endpapers: John Edward Saché, *La Martinière and the lath*,
albumen print, c. 1867.

Library of Congress Control Number: 2004100612

The Deutsche Bibliothek holds a record of this publication in
the Deutsche Nationalbibliographie; detailed bibliographical data
can be found under: http://dnb.dde.de

Prestel books are available worldwide. Please contact your
nearest bookseller or one of the above addresses for information
concerning your local distributor.

Chief editor: E. Alkazi
Editorial direction: Philippa Hurd
Typography, layout, and production: Heinz Ross, Obergries
Copyediting: Christine Davis
Proof-reading: Sarah Kane
Origination: ReproLine Genceller GmbH & Co. KG, München
Printing and Binding: Sellier Druck GmbH, Freising
Printed in Germany on acid-free paper.

ISBN: 3-7913-3130-2

Prestel Verlag
Königinstrasse 9, D-80539 Munich
Tel.: +49 (89) 38 17 09-0
Fax: +49 (89) 38 17 09-35
www.prestel.de

Prestel Publishing Ltd.
4, Bloomsbury Place, London WC1A 2QA
Tel.: +44 (020) 7323 5004
Fax: +44 (020) 7636 8004

Prestel Publishing
900 Broadway, Suite 603,
New York, N.Y. 10003
Tel.: +1 (212) 995-2720
Fax: +1 (212) 995-2733
www.prestel.com

Sepia International Inc. &
The Alkazi Collection of Photography
148 W. 24th Street, 11th floor
New York, N.Y. 10011
Tel.: +1 (212) 645-9444
Fax: +1 (212) 645-9449
e-mail: ealkazi@interport.net
www.sepia.org

43, Ovington Square
London SW3 1LJ
U. K.

M-141 Greater Kailash II
New Delhi
110 048
India

CONTENTS

List of Maps

PREFACE
ILLUSIONS OF LUCKNOW

E. Alkazi

Lucknow and Awadh (also known as Oudh) were names that conjured up, in the European imagination of the eighteenth and early nineteenth centuries, fantasies of oriental splendour and opulence. Few courts had attracted such vast numbers of merchants, travellers, artists, scholars and military adventurers from distant regions. They sought patronage and fame, and they yearned to luxuriate in the exotic lifestyle of the East.

Here, in Lucknow, was a way of life that beguiled the senses and overwhelmed them; a court that drowned itself each year in a paroxysm of grief over the recollected suffering of its religious martyrs, and, at the same time, savoured life to the full, with such finesse that its culture became a byword for refinement, courtesy and literary elegance – a reputation that continues to the present day. And all this in the midst of widespread poverty, against the backdrop of the aggressive designs of a colonialist power.

Western reactions were reflected in official reports, travel writings, works of art, and eventually, through the probing lens of the camera. Many of the East India Company's despatches with regard to the native states were critical and admonitory in tone, in order to justify its policy of annexation when there was no direct heir to the throne, or on the pretext of maladministration.

What interests us here, however, is Lucknow – the embodiment of Awadhi culture – as reflected in the city's architecture and urban design, and as seen through the eyes of nineteenth-century photographers. Most of these photographers had come in the wake of the horrific carnage and destruction that took place during the Revolt of 1857, in the course of which large sectors of a once radiant and sparkling city were reduced to rubble. Despite that, what becomes apparent – even through the lens of a frequently hostile camera – startles the viewer.

The Bara Imambara, for example, one of the architectural marvels of its time, emerges in all its nobility and grandeur (fig. 58). It was begun in 1784 by Nawab Asaf-ud-daula during a terrible famine, as a relief measure to provide income and livelihood for his starving subjects. The Husainabad Imambara (fig. 79), on a much smaller scale and totally different in concept and style, was designed by Ahmad Ali Khan, a native of Lucknow who was also a photographer of some standing. An elaborate gateway leads to a water channel flanked on one side by a handsome tomb, and on the other by a corresponding 'answering' building. The imambara, at the far end, is reflected in the water and seems to float in a tremulous shimmer of light. The patterns on its façade have the delicacy of lacework (fig. 81).

This structure is only one feature in an unusual concept of urban design. In the foreground is the Husainabad Tank, surrounded by light, graceful pavilions, and a ripple of exquisitely shaped steps that descend to the water (fig. 86). On the right, the unfinished Sat Khande, with vegetation bristling through its cracks, recalls the biblical Tower of Babel (fig. 85). In the distance, the minarets of the Jama Masjid soar into the sky like a call to prayer. In the afterglow of sunset, the atmosphere is magical.

The sweep and scale of the two-part panorama by the French nobleman Alexis de La Grange, taken around 1850, is a tribute to the feminine charm of the city, with its undulating hills, its evocative skyline of Stone Bridge, domes, minarets, spectacular gateways – all held in the embrace of the encircling river (fig. 126).

Felice Beato's 360-degree survey of the city taken in 1858 (fig. 48) is a spectacular feat of photography. Beato seemed obsessed with the idea of capturing the city in a single image of epic dimensions. What we have here is an overview of inscrutable buildings that refuse to yield their secrets to the persistent gaze of the photographer – an abandoned anthill.

To the polite visitor Lucknow responds with oriental courtesy. Shyly, she displays her waterways, her river bank with its litter of boats (fig. 124), her ancient temple in the shade of trees, John Rennie's redoubtable Iron Bridge striding across the waters (fig. 127), and the humble tomb of Boulone Lize, one of Claude Martin's seven Indian mistresses, gazing into the distance at her master's stately monument (fig. 132).

Large areas of the dream-world of the nawabs were razed to the ground after the Revolt of 1857 was ruthlessly suppressed. Nature was harnessed to cover with creepers the raw wounds of the Residency (fig. 113), and other scenes of heroic defence; cemeteries were tended with loving care, and monuments to warriors recalled their noble deeds through sacred verses and prayers in stone (fig. 118). There were no plaques to mark the sites of scores of often innocent rebel bodies strung from trees, without trial.

Comparisons between the so-called 'decadent' local Awadhi style of architecture, and that influenced by Europeans, are inevitable. Hazratganj, set up as an ideal urban thoroughfare, bears no suggestion of integrated design. We have instead a road lined on either side with commercial establishments, each trying to elbow out its equally pretentious, awkwardly proportioned neighbour. By contrast, in a side lane, we are struck by the presence of a humble native shopkeeper, disarming in his simplicity, framed in the quiet elegance of 'decadent' arches, and surrounded by his wares: containers, coils of rope, birdcages and mendicants' bowls (fig. 7).

Both the Dilkusha country house (fig. 88), based on Sir John Vanbrugh's designs for Seaton Delaval in Northumberland, and Claude Martin's La Martinière (fig. 128), seem conspicuously out of place in the Indian countryside. Sir Gore Ouseley's idea of transplanting a Northumbrian country seat into the nawab's park, however well intentioned, neither served the needs nor reflected the taste of his Indian patron. La Martinière was the architectural statement of a shrewd businessman with delusions of Napoleonic grandeur. By an irony of circumstance, Martin's tomb was vandalized by rebel sepoys during the Revolt of 1857, and his disinterred bones were flung into the river. The modest, but far more beautiful, Mughal tomb of his beloved Indian mistress remained untouched (fig. 132).

Unable to withstand the pressure of changing times, the later nawabs of Awadh turned inwards. They sequestered themselves in a realm of their own imagining, behind walls, beyond the gaze of the invader. Here, they invented a world of fantasy – with its own language, logic and meaning. Through song, dance and verse, they celebrated the senses in their subtlest nuances and variations – as the mystics, in their way, had done before. Power and glory, they realized, were illusions – the self-deceit of individuals and nations. Human beings could only come together through respect for the sanctity of life, and its collective celebration. There was no place for such a vision in the age of the Industrial Revolution, and the brutal world of international power politics.

ACKNOWLEDGEMENTS

A book such as this is, inevitably, a team effort. Each of the five contributors is indebted to the work carried out in the early stages of the project by interns working at The Alkazi Collection of Photography. Iwao Hosoda, Takahiro Kaneyama, Christine Brigid Malsbary, Preeta Nair and Rochelle Pinto all assisted with the location and identification of photographs of Lucknow on behalf of the authors. We also gratefully acknowledge the assistance of Akemi Yoneyama, Manuel Schmettau, Sayuri Rupani and Rahaab Allana. In London, we thank Stéphanie Roy for her invaluable help throughout the project.

In Lucknow, we are indebted to Professor P. C. Little, who kindly helped with the identification of photographs of Hazratganj. In Delhi we thank Mr Aslam Mahmud, who provided new information on the photographer Ahmad Ali Khan, and also the staff of Naveen Printers, Nizamuddin, who assisted with the initial design of the book.

For providing illustrations, we thank the following individuals: W. Sypniewski; Neeta Das; Giles Tillotson; Philip Stickler for the 1858 map of India, and Julie Snook who drew the two maps of Lucknow.

We are also grateful to the many museums and libraries that assisted us with the search for images of Lucknow. We thank John Falconer, Helen George, Jennifer Howes and Shashi Sen at the British Library, London; Lynne Freeman Haque and Maria Antonella Pelizzari at the Canadian Centre for Architecture, Montreal; Christie's Images, London; La Martinière College, Lucknow; Tate Britain, London; Divia Patel and Graham Parlett at the Victoria and Albert Museum, London; Victoria and Albert Museum Picture Library; and Victoria Memorial Hall, Kolkata.

For their helpful comments and suggestions on the manuscript, our thanks are due to Stanley Menezes and Uma Anand. We also thank all the staff at Prestel, in particular Philippa Hurd, Commissioning Editor in London.

Finally, a group of three people, who have worked together for many years, have each brought their individual strengths to bear on this project. Our thanks go to Esa Epstein, Executive Director of Sepia International Inc., who has given invaluable advice from the conception of the project, and is also responsible for transforming the finished manuscript into a published book; to Sophie Gordon, Associate Curator of The Alkazi Collection of Photography, without whom this book could not have been produced as she has not only provided support but also suggested and accessed many of the paintings and drawings that augment the story of Lucknow; and to Mr Ebrahim Alkazi, who originally conceived the idea of this book and approached me to edit it. Mr Alkazi's great vision is to make his remarkable collection available to the scholarly community and the general public through a series of publications. It has been both a privilege and an honour to edit the first volume.

Rosie Llewellyn-Jones

Fig. 1: Frith's Series, North-east Gate, Qaisarbagh, albumen print, mid-1870s.

INTRODUCTION

Rosie Llewellyn-Jones

For little more than eighty years the nawabi capital at Lucknow boasted the richest court in India. From its establishment in 1775 to its abrupt annexation in 1856 by the East India Company, the court blazed like a comet across the skies of northern India, and like a comet attracted all kinds of followers in its trail.

This book captures some of the physical splendour of the city during this period, reflected in its buildings, many of which no longer exist. Anyone looking at these photographs will be immediately struck by the extraordinary mixture of styles pictured here. Indeed the architecture of the city has defied most attempts at classification. It has attracted both criticism and praise, with a heavy bias towards the former. Critics have described the architecture as degenerate, tawdry and insubstantial, while admirers have defended its panache, drama and whimsicality. One cannot be indifferent to Lucknow. A brief review of the elements, both eastern and western, that contributed to the unique 'nawabi' style will offer some explanation for the hybrid buildings pictured here. But the spectator must make up his or her own mind.

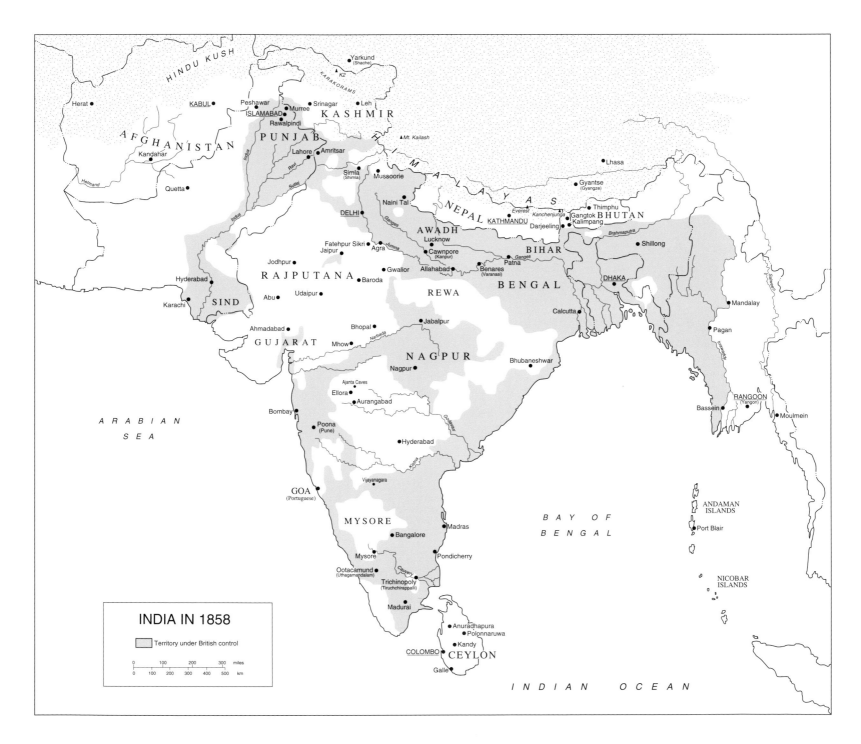

Map 1: India in 1858, indicating the extent of British control.

It was the fourth nawab, Asaf-ud-daula, who shifted the capital of Awadh from Faizabad to Lucknow in 1775. All kinds of people were attracted to the Lucknow court. There were ministers and politicians whose own origins mirrored those of the nawabs, men from good Persian backgrounds who allied themselves with their successful fellow countrymen. There were ambitious men from old-established Hindu families in Awadh, whose knowledge of financial matters, of land revenue collections, politics and the army, won them a place in the Shia nawabs' new administration. There were adventurers from Armenia and the Middle East, with their particular skills in armoury and trade. And after 1803, when Delhi, the old Mughal capital, was taken by the increasingly aggressive East India Company, there was an exodus of poets – including Mir Taqi Mir (1722–1810) and Mohammed Rafi Sauda (1713–1780) – to Lucknow. Many of these gifted but difficult men bitterly lamented the circumstances that had forced them to exchange the cultured ambience of Delhi for the parvenu court of Lucknow.

There were also, by the mid-eighteenth century, a large number of Frenchmen, soldiers and deserters from the Compagnie des Indes Orientales, who had made their way northwards after Pondicherry fell to the East India Company in 1761. Some of these men found work in the nawabs' arsenal, bringing such new skills with them that by the early 1770s it was claimed that the guns and bayonets manufactured in Lucknow were made 'almost as well as in our workshops in Europe'.[1] After these Frenchmen were dismissed in 1775 at the Company's request, their place was taken by an assortment of British adventurers, who continued to supply weapons to the nawabs from their own foundries. Others set up small businesses, importing western luxuries and novelties, like mechanical toys, through the Company's port at Calcutta. Later on there were the indigo merchants, the men who exploited this lucrative trade as a seemingly insatiable demand for the blue dye sprang up in Europe.

The majority of the European newcomers who were not in the Company's service were employed by the nawab. A very small number were employed by both. The most influential foreigner in Lucknow was Major General Claude Martin (1735–1800), a Frenchman, but one who had worked for the East India Company as a soldier since 1760. After 1775 he was also employed as superintendent in Asaf-ud-daula's arsenal. He appears in the well-known painting by Johann Zoffany, entitled *Colonel Mordaunt's Cock Match*, where he is pictured among the elite, with his employer Asaf-ud-daula (r. 1775–1797) on one side, and the British Resident, Gabriel Harper, standing behind him (fig. 2).[2] Claude Martin became an immensely rich man, whose wealth in part was founded on property and the buying, selling and renting of houses in Lucknow. He also built for himself a town house called 'Lakh-e-pera' (later renamed Farhat Bakhsh, fig. 4) and a country house that he called 'Constantia', both of which had a significant impact on the architectural development of the city during the nawabi period. Martin's long-lasting influence and his foundation of La Martinière School at Constantia are discussed in Chapter Five. (A list of all the buildings mentioned in the text is given on pp. 255–58.)

All these different elements made for a rich cultural mix, which is reflected in the buildings of Lucknow, presented here in photographs from the nineteenth century. Many of the houses that seem so English in style were not in fact inhabited by the English, although Englishmen often had a hand in their design. These were houses built for the nawabs and their nobles in the English, or European, manner. The nawabs, fairly recently arrived foreigners in India themselves, seemed enchanted by everything from the West. Their troops were drilled by European officers, their weapons, as we have seen, followed the French pattern, and their palaces often looked like English country houses, bizarrely set down on the north Indian plain. The interiors of the public rooms in the palaces were furnished in the European manner with entertainments to match, provided by the generous nawabs. Wines and liquors were imported from England, including the highly popular cherry brandy. These were served at grand European dinners, prepared by the nawabs' French cooks, and accompanied by an Anglo-Indian band, playing the latest London airs.[3]

But although on the surface the nawabs – and thus inevitably their courtiers – may have seemed Europeanized

Fig. 2: Johann Zoffany, *Colonel Mordaunt's Cock Match*, oil painting, Lucknow, 1786.

enough, even to the extent of wearing western clothes on occasion, it would be wrong to think that Awadh was a compliant ally of the East India Company. Superficial symbols of westernization may have lulled European visitors into thinking they had found something familiar so far from home, but the truth is that Lucknow was a very strange place indeed. Behind the public rooms, with their chintz sofas, Birmingham-made chandeliers and Royal Worcester dinner services, lay the womens' quarters, the *zenanas* with furnishings purely Indian in style, and intrigues, gossip, sometimes even murder. This dual tension is reflected sometimes within the same building, where the architect had to cater both for the public, western occasions and the private Indo-Persian events. These contradictions are examined in the study of Dilkusha Kothi and other 'country houses' in Chapter Three.

The Nawabi Dynasty

When the founder of the nawabi dynasty, Saadat Khan Burhan-ul-mulk (r. 1722–1739), was appointed by the Mughal court to the post of *subahdar* (governor) of Awadh, the new man had literally to fight his way into Lucknow. Awadh had descended into near anarchy as the Mughal Empire lost its hold on northern India. There were many who tried to fill the vacuum, including the Mahrattas, the Jats and the Rohillas, all increasingly powerful chieftain-led groups. The French and English East India Companies were not far behind either. In southern India independent states sprang up too, including that of Mysore, ruled by the complex and intriguing figure of Tipu Sultan, who became such a bugbear to the English Company.

In Lucknow Saadat Khan was adroit enough to establish his headquarters in the old Macchi Bhawan fort, the symbolic and actual seat of the rulers of Awadh. Members of his family and noblemen coming from the nawab's home of Nishapur in eastern Persia followed him. The new dynasty was strengthened when Saadat Khan's nephew and successor, Safdar Jung, married the first nawab's daughter.[4] By 1728

Saadat Khan was so well established that he could refuse the Delhi emperor's request to transfer him to Agra; after that it was tacitly acknowledged that the nawabs had become the autonomous rulers of Awadh. The military defeat of the third nawab, Shuja-ud-daula (r. 1754–1775), by the East India Company at Buxar in 1764, led to the start of Company interference in Awadh, and in particular to the financial penalties levied on the nawabs. But the state was still a rich prize and the nawabs used their wealth in a number of ways to emphasize their position in their new home.

Many of the customs of the old Mughal court were adopted by the earlier nawabs, who calculated correctly that this would give them the air of authority that they needed. While great emphasis was placed on nominal deference to the Mughal emperor (so long as it did not actively interfere with nawabi policy), it was now Lucknow that saw the trappings of royalty. Certainly until 1819, when the seventh nawab, Ghazi-ud-din Haider, accepted the dubious title of 'king' from the East India Company, the nawabs regarded themselves as heirs to the great Mughals. Huge hunting parties, not seen since the time of Emperor Shah Jahan, set forth every year from the nawabi palaces. The arts were actively encouraged; poets, dancers, musicians and cooks patronized; and enormous parties organized (like the wedding of Asaf-ud-daula's son, which cost £300,000 in 1795), where lakhs of rupees would literally go up in smoke, as the firework-makers strove to set the River Gomti ablaze and to emulate the old Mughal entertainments.

The Buildings of Lucknow

All traces of these ephemeral pleasures are long gone, but what does remain, and what concerns us here, is the physical legacy left behind. Nowhere is this more apparent than in the religious buildings that the nawabs and their contemporaries created. In a situation where the majority of their subjects were Hindu, and they themselves from the minority Shia sect of Islam, the nawabs quickly made Lucknow the centre of the Shia faith in northern India. They did this by a series of dramatic buildings and great complexes, rivalling the size of their palaces and pleasure gardens. Although not unique to Lucknow, the imambara, the centre of Shia ritual, especially during the month of Muharram, reached its finest form here. Chapter Two examines the most famous example, the Bara or Great Imambara, built by Asaf-ud-daula to adjoin his first home, the Macchi Bhawan palace. There were a score of other imambaras in Lucknow too, though none that covered such a great area as this most important and elaborate example. Naturally the best-endowed imambaras were those built by the nawabs, but private citizens provided money and land for smaller shrines too. Often the patron can be traced in the building's name, as in the Imambara Choti Rani ('the junior queen's imambara'), the Imambara Deputy Sahib or the Imambara Lala Jhao Lal, *lala* being here the title given to a businessman.

One of the most attractive and most photographed buildings is the Husainabad Imambara, erected by the pious nawab Muhammad Ali Shah in 1838, a year after he came to the throne. The nawab seems to have chosen a site which already contained religious buildings, for a map of 1765–66 (fig. 3) shows three substantial courtyards and mosques where the Husainabad Imambara stands today. There was also a *tripolia* (three-arched) gateway straddling the road from the city, and this may have been incorporated into the present gorgeously baroque Husainabad Gateway.

While the Bara Imambara awed the worshipper by its very size, the Husainabad Imambara is a more intimate and somehow more finished building. Standing in a large rec-

tangular courtyard, the imambara itself, on the south-west side, is reflected calmly in the waters of the central canal that runs the length of the enclosure. The imambara is well proportioned, with a central bay of five arches and a fine ribbed dome. Unlike the majority of imambaras, which rely on stucco and paint for decorative effect, the exterior of Husainabad Imambara is covered in elegant black and white calligraphic patterns.

Opposite the imambara, at the other end of the canal, with its un-Islamic, but very nawabi, statues, is an attenuated double-storeyed gateway. This is a copy of the gateway at the Dargah Hazrat Abbas, the most sacred, and oldest, Shia shrine in Lucknow.[5] In reminding pilgrims of the Dargah, the Husainabad Imambara establishes its own credentials with a respectful nod towards the past, but at the same time projects its own 'modern', highly decorated style.

The copying of buildings is something we will come across again as a distinctive feature of Lucknow architecture, both at secular and religious sites. But while the palaces and country houses realized the nawabs' dreams of Europe, the religious buildings, with their roots in Persia and Mesopotamia, confirmed the nawabs' credentials as upholders of the Shia faith in their adopted country. Although the nawabs had emigrated to India from Persia at the beginning

Fig. 3: Joseph Tieffenthaler (engraving by Kratzenstein), *Laknao*, from 'La Géographie de l'Indoustan' in J. Bernoulli's *Description historique et géographique de l'Inde*, Berlin, 1786. Drawn in 1765–66.

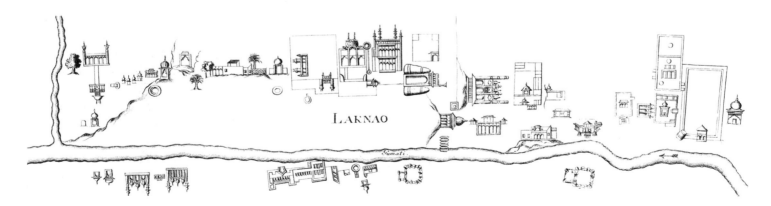

of the eighteenth century, their Persian ancestors had come from Najaf, in present-day Iraq, during the sixteenth century. Consequently the Awadh nawabs carried with them, even in India, the remembrance of their ancestral home. Their links with Mesopotamia during the period 1775–1856 were not based on a sentimental folk memory but on an active exchange of men and money. The money came from the nawabs and went to support religious endowments in Najaf and Karbala. In particular, Asaf-ud-daula paid for the construction of a new canal at Karbala, which was named after him as the Asafi Canal. Later nawabs continued to remit considerable sums of money to Karbala for the upkeep of this canal. In return, the nawabs received skilled builders from Najaf and Karbala, who were employed to re-create Shia buildings in Lucknow. (Descendants of these builders still live in the city today, a small but distinct minority.)

A few religious buildings in Lucknow are indeed promoted as copies of those in Iraq, and the Shah Najaf, the Lucknow imambara and tomb of the nawab Ghazi-ud-din Haider (r. 1814–1827), is supposedly based on a shrine in Najaf. No such building, however, can be traced today, and in fact the Shah Najaf is very much a nawabi building, despite its curious external appearance, with a shallow, Turkish-style dome (fig. 84). The only identifiable 'Iraqi' building in Lucknow is the Kazmain (fig. 83), south of the Chowk, which is a close copy of the Shrine of the Two Imams, Musa al-Kazim and Mohammed Taqi, at Kazmain, near Baghdad. The distinctive twin domes stand on deep drums rising above the flat roof of the building. The four minarets on the Lucknow shrine are less elaborately decorated than their Iraqi counterparts, but nonetheless it is a successful building, and one that would have seemed, to the inhabitants of Lucknow, equally exotic as Dilkusha Kothi, a house copied from a Palladian villa in England.

So successful were the nawabs in making Lucknow a Shia city that the numerous Hindu temples that we know were here have been quite eclipsed. Clearly they existed on the nawabs' arrival, as they do today, but very few photographs of temples, or the burning *ghats* (riverside cremation grounds) in Lucknow, seem to be known. After the trau-matic events of the Revolt of 1857 (also called the Indian Mutiny), there were British voices demanding that Lucknow be razed to the ground. Mercifully this did not happen, and although many of the palaces and country houses have subsequently been demolished, or allowed to decay, the religious buildings have, on the whole, been better cared for. It was customary for the nawab or noble who put up these structures to leave in trust a sufficient sum of money for maintenance after his death. Muhammad Ali Shah, for example, created the Husainabad Endowment Trust to support his imambara, investing a total of Rs 36 lakhs in East India Company bonds at 4% per annum.[6]

Having taken care of their souls, the nawabs turned their attention to living as luxurious a life as possible, in a series of increasingly grandiose palaces. Chapter One traces the evolution of these palaces, starting with the fortress-like Macchi Bhawan and ending with the vast, theatrical Qaisarbagh palace. The rapid changes in architectural styles, over less than a century, reflect the equally rapid changes in policy towards the nawabs by the East India Company. Between the powerful, autonomous ruler, Shuja-ud-daula, who, allied to the Mughal emperor, fought the British at Buxar in 1764, and the emasculated, tragic figure of the last nawab, Wajid Ali Shah, dethroned in 1856, the Company had moved from its trading origins to political mastery. The Company's capture of Delhi, the old Mughal capital, in 1803 symbolized the changing balance of power. The immense wealth of the nawabs attracted the greedy, impoverished Company and by the middle of the nineteenth century they had been stripped of much land and money. They had also been effectively demilitarized, the Company having undertaken to protect Awadh from outside military interference. Macchi Bhawan, a defensive, medieval palace fortress, became outdated as the nawabs moved into graceful Palladian villas, and Enlightenment ideas began to spread throughout India. Stripped of real power, but left enough money to create architectural fantasies, the later nawabs indulged in *fin de siècle* extravaganzas of building.

Alongside the nawabs' religious buildings and grandiose palaces, the third element that made up the extraordinary architectural *mélange* of Lucknow was the East India Company, although even here, things are not quite as they seem. As Chapter Four shows, the buildings in the extensive British Residency grounds were an eclectic mix of European-style houses built either by Europeans, like Claude Martin, or in the European fashion for the nawabs. There were a small number of Muslim buildings, including an old shrine, a *zenana* and a mosque. There were conventional little bungalows too, made out of locally available materials – thatch, bamboo and tiles. There was also, after 1845, a small church, one of the few buildings in the whole of the complex that the British had designed and built themselves, though even this was on land gifted by the nawab.[7] No detailed photographs are known of the Residency buildings before the Revolt of 1857. If they had existed, they would certainly have been extensively published in the aftermath of the uprising, when there was a huge outpouring of sketches, diaries, military memoirs and letters, written by those besieged for six months on the Residency hill.

Many of the photographs here are coloured by what happened in Lucknow between May 1857, when the Revolt started, and March 1858, when the British recaptured the city. Because the Revolt throughout northern India will be the subject of a separate book in this series, the topic has not

Fig. 4: Ahmad Ali Khan, working as 'Chhote Miyan', Farhat Bakhsh, Bara Chattar Manzil and adjacent palace building, albumen print, 1860.

been discussed here in detail. But for anyone seeking to re-create the Lucknow of the nawabs before annexation in 1856, the effects of the Revolt are intrusive, ranging from the mutilated north side of Qaisarbagh Palace (at first divided, then demolished) to the ruined Residency. Acres of palace buildings were demolished after 1858 on the grounds of military security. 'All the bazaar was cleared away', wrote a woman who had been a royal maid-servant. 'The English like grass better than bazaars.'[8]

A few precious photographs exist from before the British clearances, however. Ahmad Ali Khan, architect, superintendent and court photographer to the last nawab, Wajid Ali Shah (r. 1847–1856), gamely climbed on to the roofs of Chattar Manzil and Dilaram Kothi with his camera one day in 1855/56 and produced a few panoramic rooftop views.[9] There also exists a fascinating series of stereoscopic photographs, meant to be viewed through a stereoscope to give a three-dimensional image. From internal evidence these appear to have been taken by a photographer immediately after the recapture of the city on 15 March 1858, before the debris of battle was cleared away.[10] In these haunting images, the city seems to be waiting for retribution after its fall to the British. The photographer wandered freely around the city, from the grounds of La Martinière (fig. 132) to the rooftops of the Chattar Manzil palace. How evocative these early pictures are, and how splendid must have been Lucknow before the fall.

Mapping the City

Some of the earliest maps of Lucknow were collected by the East India Company's historian, Robert Orme, in the late eighteenth century.[11] Like other Indian maps of the period, these were drawn to indicate the route between different cities, and because these schematic maps are labelled in English, they were almost certainly produced for East India Company officials to enable them to direct their palanquin bearers on the stages of their journeys. (Anyone who has travelled by rickshaw, tonga or taxi in India will appreciate

the importance of knowing where they are going, even if their driver doesn't.)

The most detailed map (1767) traces the route to the Ganges, via the large town of Purva. It shows Lucknow as a town of some considerable size, built up for almost two miles south of the Gomti and stretching for over two miles from east to west. The Macchi Bhawan fort, then being beautified by Nawab Shuja-ud-daula, is the most prominent building. Although the Stone Bridge is not indicated, the road starts from what would be the southern end of the bridge, skirts the Panch Mahalla Gateway, drawn by Thomas Daniell some twenty years later (fig. 13), and proceeds in a south-westerly direction through the Chowk. The various *mohallas* (neighbourhoods), though not named, are shown as distinct areas, separated by paths, radiating out from the fort.

An undated, but circa 1767, map shows the road from Faizabad to Lucknow, an important and well-travelled route, as the nawabs and their retinue moved between the two towns. This map, in a book of route marches, which Robert Orme acquired in 1773, shows that north Lucknow, across the River Gomti, had already started to develop by this time. Mukarimnagar and Mahanagar, now only district names in the sprawl of modern Lucknow, were then distinct villages. Intriguingly, Lakh-e-pera Garden, associated with Claude Martin, is shown as an area north of the river. Today's Faizabad road follows the old route fairly closely, striking due east across the little Kukrail river.

Infuriatingly there seem to be no maps extant for the period between 1775 and late 1857. Until Lucknow's annexation in February 1856, the officials of the East India Company, housed on the Residency hill, were regarded as 'guests' by successive nawabs. Although they were highly unusual 'guests', frequently criticizing their 'host' and demanding that he modify his behaviour, even the Residents realized that they could not openly survey the capital city of a supposedly autonomous kingdom. The Residency newswriters, a euphemism for spies, reported daily on events in the city, and it is inconceivable that the Residency offices did not

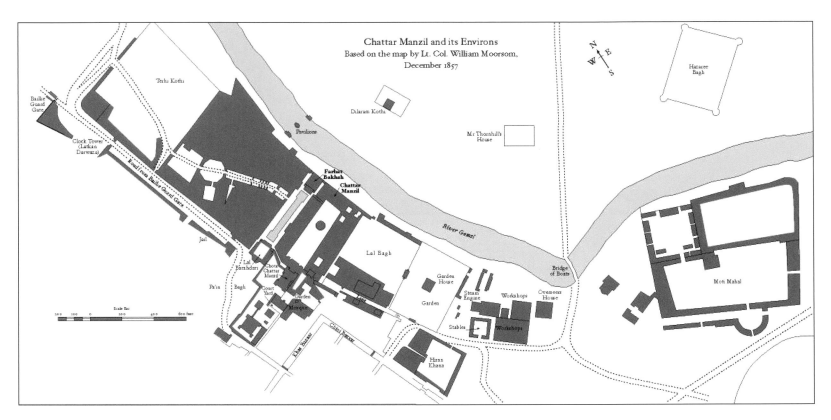

Map 3: Chattar Manzil and its Environs, Based on the map by Lt. Col. William Moorsom, December 1857.

ingly, had actually restored the straight line of Saadat Ali Khan's great Hazratganj road, which had been diverted by later additions to Chattar Manzil palace. After 1858, instead of making a diversion around the palace walls and regaining the road by walking diagonally across the garden in front of the Lal Barahdari, the townspeople could once again travel on the old road straight up to the battered Baillie Guard Gate, the entrance to the now ruined Residency.

The Residency itself was included in the 1857 map by Lt. Col. William Moorsom, and this was thereafter frequently reproduced in memoirs and accounts of the siege. The map naturally gives the names of the buildings used during the siege, for this is what readers were interested in. We do not have all the original names of these buildings, although we know many of the people who lived here during the eighty-odd years of the Residency's inhabitation. What Moorsom's map shows is not only the line of entrenchments, following the street pattern around the hill, and frantically reinforced by the British as they prepared themselves for the siege, but more interestingly, the proximity of the houses surrounding the hill. To the south and west, the 'native houses' shown on the map were only the width of a street away, and this now makes sense of contemporary statements that the 'mutineers' were standing at the windows of these houses and firing directly into the Residency buildings.

Picturing the City

It is not surprising that the dazzling new buildings and colourful personalities of Lucknow attracted artists from both East and West. In 1772, while the court of Awadh was

Fig. 5: Lucknow artist after Tilly Kettle, *Shuja-ud-daula and his Ten Sons,* oil painting, c. 1815.

Fig. 6: William Carpenter, *Ganj and Tripolia Gateway near the Macchi Bhawan,* pencil and watercolour, c. 1856.

Fig. 7: Edmund David Lyon, Shopkeeper, albumen print, c. 1862.

Fig. 10: John Edward Saché, North end of the Jilau Khana, Qaisarbagh, with the Tombs of Saadat Ali Khan and Begum Khurshid Zadi beyond, albumen print, c. 1867.

Chapter One

THE ROYAL PALACES

Sophie Gordon

It is all too easy when considering the nawabi residences of Lucknow to let the vision of the remains of Qaisar-bagh Palace, the last nawabi construction on any great scale, cloud our understanding of the buildings that came before it. The theatrical and ephemeral qualities of Qaisar-bagh are usually seen as the culmination of one hundred years of steady decline into 'grotesqueness', starting from a point that was already well past the peak of Mughal achievement.[1] Yet with an effort of imagination, we can see Lucknow as it was seen by those who visited the court in the eighteenth and early nineteenth centuries – a court that from the 1750s onwards was located in a palace built around an old Sheikh-zada fort, known as Macchi Bhawan.[2] The main palace building, which was situated inside the walls of Macchi Bhawan fort, was known as Panch Mahalla. It was constructed and enlarged during the reign of Safdar Jung (r. 1739–1754) and his successor Shuja-ud-daula (r. 1754–1775), making it contemporary with the Qudsia Bagh Palace in Delhi.[3] Macchi Bhawan remained the principal royal residence until the late 1780s, when Asaf-ud-daula (r. 1775–1797) built the sprawling collection of buildings known as Daulat Khana. In the early years of the nineteenth century, Saadat Ali Khan

(r. 1798–1814) built Chattar Manzil and made it the principal nawabi residence until the construction of Qaisarbagh, which was completed in 1852, during the reign of Wajid Ali Shah.

These four royal residences were used by the nawabs until 1856 when Wajid Ali Shah was deposed by the British and went to live in Calcutta with the remnants of his court. Other, less significant, palaces were constructed during the nawabi period, most notably the Moti Mahal (c. 1798–1800). Commissioned by Saadat Ali Khan and later enlarged by Ghazi-ud-din Haider, Moti Mahal was positioned on the river's edge and consisted of at least three major courtyards with a prominent gateway (fig. 18).[4] There was, furthermore, Matiya Burj Palace in Calcutta, the home of the exiled nawab. One commentator described it as 'an earthly paradise'.[5] In its time Matiya Burj, located close to the Botanical Gardens, was a vast complex of houses and gardens, but today what remains of it is used as offices by the railway department.[6]

This chapter is a survey of the visual material illustrating the four main palace complexes: Macchi Bhawan, Daulat Khana, Chattar Manzil and Qaisarbagh. As most of the physical evidence for these structures has almost completely disappeared, or been altered beyond recognition, it is only through the prints, paintings and drawings that we can start to reconstruct a clearer history of these buildings. It is surprisingly rare for architectural historians to examine such visual material in their work, although Régine Thiriez's relatively recent study of the Chinese Imperial Summer Palace has shown that a thorough investigation of photographic evidence, alongside the surviving remains of the buildings, can produce significant findings for both photo-historians and architectural historians.[7]

Macchi Bhawan

The missionary Father Joseph Tieffenthaler, who visited Lucknow in 1765–66, has left the earliest description of the Macchi Bhawan:

'The main building is undoubtedly that which is known as the Panch Mahal, which lies a short distance from the Gomti alongside its riverbank, on raised ground; [it is] built as a fort, surrounded by walls and high towers. There is a tall gateway and a large courtyard, which stands before a tall arcaded building, designed for the playing of drums.'[8]

In the accompanying illustration (fig. 11), which was engraved by a Monsieur Kratzenstein after Tieffenthaler's own sketches, the 'tall gateway' (generally known as the Panch Mahalla Gateway) is clearly shown, flanked by two large bastions. In front are the courtyard and the building known as the *naubat khana*, the place where drums and other instruments are played to mark certain times of the day or the arrival of particular visitors. The *naubat khana* is a traditional feature of the Mughal palace; a similar example still exists in Shah Jahan's Lal Qila (Red Fort) in Delhi.[9]

The Panch Mahalla and its surroundings are best known today from the extraordinary eight-part panorama of Lucknow made in April 1858 by Felice Beato (fig. 48). Taken from a minaret of the Asafi Mosque it encompasses much of the eastern part of the city, which was developed by the nawabs in the early nineteenth century. The central section shows what remained of the oldest part of the city after the Revolt of 1857: the ruins of Macchi Bhawan, with the *tripolia* gate, and the Panch Mahalla Gateway.

The *naubat khana* at Macchi Bhawan was a *tripolia* gateway, which stood at the eastern end of a busy *ganj* (market street). At the opposite end of the *ganj* was a second, identical gateway. The road in between the gateways would have been lined with busy shops (fig. 6). The gateway at the western end of the *ganj* was subsequently incorporated into the forecourt of Asaf-ud-daula's Bara Imambara and mosque complex, and was renamed Rumi Darwaza. The older structure within the Rumi Darwaza can be seen clearly in a photograph from the late 1860s (fig. 53).

The visitors who successfully negotiated their way through the *naubat khana* and the first courtyard would then be faced with the Panch Mahalla Gateway. Thomas Daniell, who was in Lucknow between July and October of 1789, produced an aquatint of this gate showing the bastions and heavy massing on either side of the entrance (fig. 13). The impressive size of the gateway, or at least the Daniells' perception of it, is indicated by the comparatively small elephant that cautiously approaches.

Tieffenthaler's plan of Macchi Bhawan also highlights these tall bastions placed at regular intervals along the external walls, a distinctive feature of the fort which would have struck anyone approaching it from the River Gomti (fig. 12). These bastions can be seen in several paintings and photographs, and provide us with a point of reference against which to mark subsequent architectural changes. In William Hodges' view of Macchi Bhawan the bastions are clearly visible (fig. 14).[10] Above them rises Panch Mahalla itself, which on this occasion, at least, failed to impress. Hodges, who visited the city in 1783, wrote:

'The palace of the Nabob is on a high bank, near to the river, and commanding an extensive view both of the Goomty and the country on the eastern side. ... The exterior of the building is not to be commended: it reminded me of what I had imagined might be the style of a Baron's castle in Europe, about the twelfth century.'[11]

Both Hodges' and the Daniells' views reflect some of the changes that had taken place within Macchi Bhawan during Asaf-ud-daula's occupancy. There were by now additional descending levels of courtyards, each containing gardens and pavilions. The most important of these was the Sungi Dalan (Stone Hall), described thus in 1785:

'[It] comprises a grand hall, surrounded with a double arcade, crowned with four cupolas at the corners, and one at the principal front, covered with copper doubly gilt. At the extremities of the terrace are two wings, for morning and evening resort. From both fronts extends a long flower garden divided into parterres by walks and fountains... Within the precinct of the gardens is also a small mosque, with gilt minars, commodious offices and swings for ladies' exercise.'[12]

Following the departure of the nawab in 1789, Macchi Bhawan was by no means left deserted. Relatives and important members of the court would often occupy the older palace buildings. When George Annesley (later Viscount Valentia) visited Lucknow in 1803 with the artist Henry Salt, they found Macchi Bhawan occupied by the mother of Saadat Ali Khan. The palace was beginning to show its age:

'I had paid his Excellency the Vizier the compliment of first visiting his own mother ... She resides in the zenana of his palace, a building going rapidly to decay and without any beauty.'[13]

The building survived nevertheless. Similar views to those of Hodges and Salt, dating to the first half of the nineteenth century, show Macchi Bhawan still in a reasonable condition. A slightly later description written in 1858 by Martin Gubbins, the Financial Commissioner of Awadh, portrays the fort as it was immediately before fighting broke out in 1857:

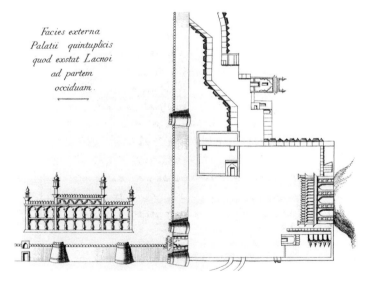

Fig. 11: Joseph Tieffenthaler (engraving by Kratzenstein), *Facies externa Palatii quintuplicis* [Panch Mahalla], from 'La Géographie de l'Indoustan' in J. Bernoulli's *Description historique et géographique de l'Inde*, Berlin, 1786. Drawn in 1765–66.

'It comprises three plateaus, of which the lowest was a little above the level of the road, and the highest towered above the neighbouring buildings … The highest plateau was covered with the 'bhowuns' or pavilions originally built by the Sheikhs of Lucknow … On the second plateau stood a handsome baraduree … The lower plateau was an open square surrounded by the low ranges of masonry sheds.'[14]

Macchi Bhawan had in fact been occupied by the British in 1856, after Wajid Ali Shah was deposed, but the situation changed suddenly following the outbreak of hostilities in June 1857. The Chief Commissioner of Awadh, Sir Henry Lawrence, had initially decided to use Macchi Bhawan as a defensible stronghold for the British community but his Sappers persuaded him that it would be easy for the enemy to lay mines beneath the foundations. Lawrence therefore decided to withdraw the troops and remove everyone to the Residency. On 1 July 1857 a message was sent by semaphore from the tower of the Residency to the few remaining soldiers at the fort: 'Spike the guns well, blow up the fort and retire at midnight.'[15] The men followed their instructions and abandoned the fort, which was subsequently occupied by rebel Indian troops.

In March 1858 the British recaptured Lucknow. Accompanying the troops in the wake of their progress through the city was Felice Beato. His panorama (fig. 48) shows that some elements of Macchi Bhawan survived. The *tripolia*

gate and the Panch Mahalla Gateway can be seen on the road near the river (fig. 48, part 5).

It has been assumed that shortly after this, the fort was entirely destroyed.[16] Sir Robert Napier of the Royal Engineers had produced a new plan for the city within a week of his arrival in Lucknow in March 1858. He recommended widespread clearances, particularly in the old city, to allow for the building of new roads and to improve defensive capabilities. Napier's plans were swiftly approved, and many buildings were pulled down over the next twenty years as engineers strove to fulfil his vision. Macchi Bhawan, however, survived. In fact, Napier had recommended that a large *maidan* be created around the fort, similar to the area cleared around Lal Qila in Delhi in the same year.[17]

The ruins of the fort were quickly repaired in order to put the building to use as a military depot. A photograph taken in 1860 illustrates the remarkable extent of the restorations (fig. 15). The *tripolia* gate seems to have disappeared at this stage, however, as it does not appear in any photograph or painting post-1860. It also seems likely that some of the

Fig. 12: Joseph Tieffenthaler (engraving by Kratzenstein), *Palatium quod Laknoi visitum ripae Gumatis adstium* [Macchi Bhawan], from 'La Géographie de l'Indoustan' in J. Bernoulli's *Description historique et géographique de l'Inde*, Berlin, 1786. Drawn in 1765–66.

Fig. 13: Thomas Daniell, *The Punj Mahalla Gate, Lucnow* [The Panch Mahalla Gateway, Macchi Bhawan, Lucknow], July–October 1789, Plate 5 from *Oriental Scenery*, vol. III, aquatint, published 1801.

Fig. 14: William Hodges (engraving by James Fittler), *A View of the Palace of Nabob Asoph ul Dowlah at Lucknow* [Macchi Bhawan], from *Travels in India during the Years 1780, 1781, 1782 and 1783*, London, 1793.

more outlying sections of the palace were dismantled at this time.

In 1874, Abbas Ali (or Darogha Ubbas Alli, as he styled himself), the Assistant Municipal Engineer of the city, described Macchi Bhawan as 'a fort of considerable strength armed with heavy guns, and garrisoned by both artillery and infantry'.[18] It survived for about another ten years, but by 1891 it had been demolished:

'His [Asaf-ud-daula's] fort, noticeable for its round earthern bastions and famous for its strength, was demolished some years ago for strategic reasons.'[19]

Any last remaining traces of the fort were finally cleared away in 1912 when the King George and Queen Mary's Hospital and College, designed by Samuel Swinton Jacob, was built on the site. The name 'Macchi Bhawan' still lingers, however, as it is sometimes used by inhabitants of Lucknow to describe this particular area of the city.

Daulat Khana

Of all the Lucknow palaces, Daulat Khana remains today the most elusive. In 1789 Asaf-ud-daula moved into a new building here, which was named Asafi Kothi ('House of Asaf', fig. 89). At the same time, other pavilions were still being constructed. Few outsiders were invited to visit during the nawabi period, so written descriptions are sparse. Some sketches of the area were made by Captain Robert Smith in March 1832 (fig. 16), but what evidence survives for Daulat Khana comes largely from photographs that were made in 1858, after many of the buildings had been damaged or destroyed. Beato's two-part panorama taken from the Jama Masjid shows the Husainabad Imambara complex; on the far left of the photograph, the buildings of Daulat Khana appear as they stood in April 1858 (fig. 71).

Passing through the gateway decorated with a pair of 'nawabi' fish, which stands just beyond the tower of Sat Khande in Beato's panorama, one encountered Gol Kothi, a building constructed in a classical European style. Surrounded by a high wall and many trees, it has a curved portico at the front. On the side of the house a classical pediment is visible. Beyond this, partly hidden by the trees, is Asafi Kothi. It is a two-storeyed building, with architectural features that derive from the western classical tradition, such as the round arches and the double composite columns. This contrasts with the religious buildings being constructed in Lucknow at this time, which are entirely late Mughal in conception.[20] Today, Asafi Kothi is in poor condition, although some descendants of Nawab Muhammad Ali Shah and Nawab Wajid Ali Shah, the last ruler of Lucknow, still live there.

The only structures that have survived in good condition are the stepped tank and the building known today as the Picture Gallery. There is no description outlining the original purpose of the tank or the Picture Gallery, but it is probable that the tank was used for entertainment purposes, with the audience watching from the arcaded gallery that overlooks the water. A photograph made in around 1867 provides a closer view of the tank and its pavilions (fig. 85).

To the right of the tank in Beato's two-part panorama stands a prominent building with a long sloping roof. This is the Gend Khana, used as a racket court. References to racket courts in Lucknow include mention of a second one in the British Residency complex. The example seen here may

Fig. 15: Donald Horne Macfarlane, Macchi Bhawan after restoration, albumen print, c. 1860.

Fig. 16: Captain Robert Smith, Panorama of Lucknow showing the Daulat Khana palace, eight pencil sketches, 1832.

have been constructed during the nawabi period, but it is also possible that it was a British building dating from 1856, as Daulat Khana palace was occupied by the British between 1856 and 1858. The Gend Khana was destroyed in around 1860.[21] Next to the Gend Khana there was a second Macchi Darwaza (Fish Gateway). This gateway is almost certainly the same as that seen in Smith's 1832 drawing (fig. 16).

After the death of Asaf-ud-daula in 1797, Saadat Ali Khan moved into Daulat Khana and also built himself 'The New Palace' in this area.[22] Shortly afterwards he moved into a town house further downstream, which had belonged to Claude Martin. This house, which the nawab renamed 'Farhat Bakhsh', was the beginning of the Chattar Manzil palace.

Chattar Manzil

Chattar Manzil was, in the early nineteenth century, a large and impressive palace complex that dazzled visitors. It lived up to European preconceptions of what an Indian palace really should be. Emily Eden, sister of the Governor General, wrote:

'Such a place! The only residence I have coveted in India. Don't you remember reading in the Arabian Nights, Zobeide bets her Garden of Delight against the Caliph's Palace of Pictures! I am sure this was the Garden of Delight.'[23]

Chattar Manzil consisted of several distinct buildings and gardens, including Farhat Bakhsh, the Lal Barahdari, Bara (Great) Chattar Manzil and Chota (Lesser) Chattar Manzil. The few buildings that survive today present a very different picture from the complex that developed here over a period of forty years or so, between 1780 and 1820, containing apartments, pavilions, mosques, tanks and gardens.

Farhat Bakhsh

Claude Martin's town house (fig. 17), known during his lifetime as Lakh-e-pera, was completed in 1781, according to an inscription over a basement arch. The house was one of the earliest that Claude Martin designed in Lucknow, preceding both Constantia and Bibiapur, and as such was to have a great influence on subsequent nawabi designs.[24]

Farhat Bakhsh could be approached either from the river or by land from the south, where the visitor had to cross a drawbridge that was lowered over the moat. One then passed through a large courtyard, eventually reaching a large octagonal room from which there was access to several smaller rooms. There were two principal floors above ground, with octagonal pavilions on the roof. There were also two storeys below ground level. These floors, known as *tykhanas*, were used during the summer months to escape the heat. Once the rains arrived, the water level would begin to rise and one would be forced to ascend above ground level. The *tykhanas* can just be glimpsed in early photographs (fig. 4) and are still visible today, although they are now permanently flooded.

This small fortress of a house was substantially altered when Saadat Ali Khan purchased the building after the death of Claude Martin in 1800. The moat and drawbridge disappeared, and a tank was placed on the south side of the building (see Map 3). Two buildings were situated to the west of Farhat Bakhsh. The first unnamed, immediately adjacent building was demolished by 1860 (fig. 4). The second building, known as the Summer Palace, survived until the late nineteenth century, although its outlying structures were demolished in 1858. Seen in an early photograph are the remnants of pavilions in the Gomti that 'bridged' the Summer Palace and Dilaram Kothi (fig. 122).[25] In 1874, Abbas Ali described the pavilions as 'water temples' where, in the evening, the nawab would 'sit in the centre one, in the cool of the evening and fish with rod and line … those on the banks have disappeared entirely, and all that remains of the centre one, is the masonry pier upon which it stood' (fig. 123).[26]

South of the Farhat Bakhsh, at the end of the tank, was another of Saadat Ali Khan's new constructions, known as Qasrul Khakan (King's House), or more familiarly as Lal Barahdari (Red Pavilion). It was built to serve as the *durbar* hall of the nawabs (fig. 26). Abbas Ali decided that, 'leaving religion out of the question, it may be considered the "Westminster Abbey" of Oudh. It was the Throne Room, the Coronation Hall and Grand Durbar of Halls of Assembly of the Monarchs of Oudh.'[27] The bricks are covered with a thick red plaster, hence the name of the building. The red plaster imitates the red sandstone that was used in the imperial palaces of Fatehpur Sikri, Agra and Delhi, which came to be associated with imperial authority. For many years Lal Barahdari housed the Lucknow Provincial Museum. Today the building is part of an art college and the *durbar* hall is used for exhibitions.

Bara Chattar Manzil

Saadat Ali Khan was responsible for the construction of Bara Chattar Manzil (c. 1800–14), a symmetrical four-

storeyed building situated at the edge of the river, which became the main building in the complex (fig. 29). As at Farhat Bakhsh, there was a courtyard on the south side of the building with a range of smaller courtyards extending along at least one side. In the centre of the courtyard there was a large, round, single storey pavilion. This unusual structure, known only through a single photograph, had around its circumference what appear to be *jalis* (perforated screens). It is difficult to speculate on the use of such a pavilion, but it may have been devoted to some sort of entertainment, possibly a diorama. Such entertainments were certainly known in Lucknow during the early nineteenth century. In 1818, the artist Robert Home described 'a building for Panoramas' that he was designing, which would allow spectators to remain seated while the panoramas revolved around them.[28]

During 1857–58 Bara Chattar Manzil came under heavy fire, sustaining a great deal of damage. After the British reasserted control of Lucknow in March 1858, the building was quickly restored in a matter of months, as was the case with Macchi Bhawan.[29] The restoration involved the demolition of the south courtyard and its replacement with

Fig. 17:
William Hodges
(engraving by Morris),
View of a House built by Col. Claude Martin at Lucknow, 1790,
published in *The European Magazine and London Review*, based on
a drawing of 1782.

grass and trees (fig. 30). The *chattri* destroyed in 1857 was replaced, and the dome on the highest level was repaired and given a golden finial. Similarly, all traces of the buildings to the south of Farhat Bakhsh were completely removed.

After 1858, the larger Chattar Manzil was for many years the home of the United Services Club, incorporating a hotel and 'a most elegant restaurant, delightfully cool in summer'.[30] Today the building houses the Central Drug Research Institute and is partially concealed from public view by a large wall.

Chota Chattar Manzil

To the south of Bara Chattar Manzil, Ghazi-ud-din Haider constructed in 1814–27 a group of three large buildings which were huddled closely together, next to the Lal Barah-dari, known as Chota Chattar Manzil, Gulistan-i-Iram ('Rose Garden of Paradise') and Darshan Bilas ('Delightful Aspect'; fig. 20). They were surrounded by numerous other palace buildings, as well as a cluster of small mosques and an imambara. Early photographs indicate how built-up the area was before the demolitions of 1858–60.[31] A later photograph from 1864/65 shows clearly the relative positioning of the different elements within the Chattar Manzil complex after the clearances and later restoration work (fig. 19). A large tank with a small island in the middle originally separated Bara and Chota Chattar Manzil. This was the scene of many spectacular parties and firework displays in the nineteenth century.

Chota Chattar Manzil, topped by a golden dome with a *chattri*, sat in the middle of the two other buildings (fig. 27). Approaching it from the south, one passed through a portico before arriving in a large octagonal room, with spiral staircases on either side which led up to the next level. The south façade of the building (the side most commonly photographed in the nineteenth century) makes heavy use of European architectural features. By contrast, the north façade, rarely photographed, employed only Islamic features common to an imambara, the principal front of which

faced north.[32] After 1858 the building was home to public service offices. It was later used as a club and also as a library before it collapsed rather suddenly in the 1970s, apparently due to subsidence.

Gulistan-i-Iram and Darshan Bilas

Gulistan-i-Iram and Darshan Bilas stood either side of Chota Chattar Manzil. These two fairly substantial buildings were constructed in around 1828–32. Gulistan-i-Iram has two large floors with a third, pavilion-esque, storey above. The main, east-facing entrance has a classical Ionic portico with a pediment. Other features, such as blind rounded arches and stucco ornamentation, are also freely employed. The original use of the building is not known, but after 1858 it housed the law courts before these moved to their new site opposite Lal Barahdari. By 1904 it was occupied by a branch of the Provincial Museum. Although the museum has since moved out, the building still exists today.

Darshan Bilas is one of the most peculiar and extraordinary buildings in Lucknow (fig. 21). Consisting of four wings surrounding a courtyard, each of the outward-facing façades copies the façade of a well-known building in the city. The east front resembles Farhat Bakhsh; the west front copies Dilkusha Kothi (figs. 22 & 23) and the north and south façades both imitate Barowen (also known as Musa Bagh (figs. 24 & 25). The copies are not exact, but they are close enough to be readily identified. Because of this, the building is sometimes referred to by the name Chaurukhi Kothi, which means 'House of Four Faces'. No specific use is known for these buildings, collectively referred to as the Chota Chattar Manzil complex. The European-style interiors give little in the way of information, although it has been suggested that one of the *kothis* would have been for the women of the court.

Chattar Manzil palace remained the principal royal residence until the accession of Wajid Ali Shah in 1847. The construction of Qaisarbagh Palace began the following year, being interpreted by some as an attempt to escape from the European influence – so evident in Chattar Manzil and the earlier Daulat Khana – towards something that followed more consciously an Islamic tradition.[33] In fact Qaisarbagh, whatever the intentions of the nawab, was to be a hybrid construction, combining Indian and European features and motifs side by side.

Fig. 18: Darogha Ubbas Alli, Gateway to the Moti Mahal, Plate 16 from *The Lucknow Album*, albumen print, c. 1870, published 1874.

Fig. 19: Samuel Bourne, Looking west towards the Chattar Manzil complex, albumen print, December 1864–early 1865.

Fig. 20: J. C. A. Dannenberg, Gulistan-i-Iram (left), Chota Chattar Manzil (centre) and Darshan Bilas (right), albumen print, c. 1860.

Fig. 21: Samuel Bourne, Darshan Bilas and Chota Chattar Manzil, albumen print, December 1864–early 1865.

Fig. 22: Samuel Bourne, Western façade of Darshan Bilas, albumen print (detail of fig. 21), December 1864–early 1865.

Fig. 23: Felice Beato, Façade of Dilkusha Kothi, albumen print (detail of fig. 104), 1858.

Fig. 24: Samuel Bourne, Southern façade of Darshan Bilas, albumen print (detail of fig. 21), December 1864–early 1865.

Fig. 25: Felice Beato, Rear façade of Barowen, also known as Musa Bagh, albumen print (detail of fig. 101), 1858.

Fig. 26: John Edward Saché, Lal Barahdari, albumen print, c. 1867.

Fig. 27: John Edward Saché, Chota Chattar Manzil, albumen print, c. 1867

Fig. 28: John Edward Saché, Bara Chattar Manzil from the River Gomti, with the Chota Chattar Manzil and Darshan Bilas beyond, albumen print, c. 1867.

Fig. 29:
John Edward Saché,
Bara Chattar Manzil
from the River
Gomti,
albumen print,
c. 1867

Clearly seen in
this photograph is
a large hall to the left
of the main palace.
Not visible in
photographs from
the early 1860s,
it was destroyed
during the Revolt
of 1857 and rebuilt
in the mid-1860s.

Fig. 30: Shepherd & Robertson, Bara Chattar Manzil and Farhat Bakhsh, south side, albumen print, c. 1862.

Qaisarbagh Palace

Under the direction of the designer Ahmad Ali Khan,[34] the construction of Qaisarbagh was relatively swift. Beginning in 1848, the palace was finished by 1852 when Wajid Ali Shah installed himself. Very few visitors were allowed inside; consequently both written and visual accounts describing life in the palace during the nawab's brief occupancy are rare. One of the earliest views is an unusual painting from the early 1850s which shows Wajid Ali Shah leading a procession into the Jilau Khana (central courtyard) of Qaisarbagh.[35] By far the best single document for Qaisarbagh, however, is a six-part panoramic photograph of the complex by Felice Beato (fig. 32) which, moving from west to east, incorporates the secondary courtyards, the surrounding apartment buildings (which were destroyed between 1859 and 1865) and the Jilau Khana.

The Jilau Khana is the only part of the palace that still remains readily identifiable today, yet nearly everything that originally stood within its walls has vanished. Only the Safaid Barahdari ('White Barahdari'), today known as the Taluqdars' Hall, still occupies its position in the centre of the courtyard (fig. 33). Constructed as an imambara, its proper name is Qasrul Aza, meaning 'house of mourning'.[36] Alterations have been made to the building over the years, including the addition of a second storey.

Several of the structures originally in the Jilau Khana were built purely for entertainment purposes, such as the Lanka, an architectural folly which stood at the south end of the courtyard (figs. 34–37). The central bridge, decorated with a pair of fish, passed over a small raised pavilion; additional pavilions originally sat on the roof of either wing.[37] The Lanka was destroyed in around 1911 to make way for the Amir-ud-daula Public Library.

On either side of the Lanka in each of the southernmost corners of the Jilau Khana were raised platforms with pavilions on them, visible in Beato's panorama. The platforms had octagonal towers at each corner and were enclosed by pillars. The pavilions disappeared in around 1860, but the pillars surrounding them survived for a few more years. They can be seen in photographs of 1862–63, but they too had vanished by the late 1860s. Beato's panorama also shows in the foreground one of the four large vines that grew in the Jilau Khana (fig. 35). The vines had all disappeared by around 1870. Moving north across the courtyard, one found a pair of mosques and further pavilions situated within small, cultivated gardens. Statues on plinths stood around the edges of these gardens (fig. 45). The majority of the statues were European, or at least copies from European models, and were much derided by European visitors.[38]

To the north of the *barahdari* were more gardens, which featured a number of bird perches on poles. Running along the north-south axis was a short water channel; if followed, this would eventually lead the visitor over a small bridge, crossing another water channel, running east-west. The bridge, known as the Fairy Bridge, was decorated with mermen. At either end of the east–west channel were houses; the eastern house was known as the Tosha Khana (a furniture store, or store room). Tantalizing glimpses of these houses can be seen in Beato's panorama, although it is very difficult to distinguish them from the enclosure walls. Both the houses were in poor condition following the siege of 1858 and were demolished shortly after. Running off the side of the houses were colonnaded walkways, which are thought to have been pigeon houses. At least one of these survived independently of its house until the late 1860s (fig. 33).

In the centre of the east and west walls of the courtyard stand the grand gateways, directly opposite each other, emblazoned with serpentine mermaids and fish motifs on both sides (figs. 38 & 39). The quadrant arches which top both gates are copies of those found on the roof of Claude Martin's house, Constantia. Both of these gateways have survived, but are today shadows of their former selves.

Many of the pavilions and other structures that have disappeared from the Jilau Khana were removed as part of Napier's post-1858 clearance and restoration programme. The gardens were also frequently rearranged. A road was driven through Qaisarbagh in around 1861, cutting across the north-eastern corner of the square and exiting through

Fig. 31: Lucknow School, *A Hunting Procession near the Stone Bridge*, pencil and watercolour heightened with body colour, c. 1820.

Fig. 32: Felice Beato, The courtyards of the Qaisarbagh from the Roshan-ud-daula Kothi, six albumen prints, 1858

Taken from the roof of Roshan-ud-daula Kothi, the view shows the Jilau Khana at the centre of the Qaisarbagh and the surrounding courtyards. At the centre of the Jilau Khana is a white *barahdari*, actually an imambara, more properly known as Qasrul Aza. The large dome at the forefront of the panorama is part of Roshan-ud-daula Kothi.

Fig. 33: John Edward Saché, The Safaid Barahdari and the 'Pigeon House' (on the far right) in the Jilau Khana, Qaisarbagh, albumen print, c. 1867.

Fig. 34: Unknown photographer, The Lanka in the Jilau Khana, Qaisarbagh, albumen print, 1860s.

Fig. 35: Shepherd & Robertson, The Great Vine and the Lanka, Qaisarbagh, albumen print, c. 1862.

Fig. 36: John Edward Saché, The Lanka, Qaisarbagh, albumen print, c. 1867.

Fig. 37: Frith's Series, The Lanka, Qaisarbagh, albumen print, mid-1870s.

Fig. 42: Samuel Bourne, Roshan-ud-daula Kothi, albumen print, December 1864–early 1865.

Fig. 43: Frith's Series, Roshan-ud-daula Kothi, south side, mid-1870s.

Fig. 44: Frith's Series, Roshan-ud-daula Kothi, north side, albumen print, 1870s.

Fig. 45:
Samuel Bourne,
The Jilau Khana,
Qaisarbagh,
with the Tombs
of Saadat Ali Khan
and Begum
Khurshid Zadi,
albumen print,
December
1864–early 1865.

Fig. 46: Robert Tytler and Harriet Tytler, attrib., Tomb of Saadat Ali Khan, albumen print, c. 1858.

Fig. 47: Frith's Series, Tomb of Begum Khurshid Zadi, albumen print, 1870s.

Felice Beato's Panorama of the Great Imambara, 1858

E. Alkazi

An eerie silence, that of a graveyard, hangs over the sequence of eight shots that comprise Beato's far-ranging view, taken from one of the minarets of the Asafi Mosque within the precincts of the Great Imambara (fig. 48).

This wide and sweeping coverage which shows some of the city's sectors might easily depict craters on the moon's surface, so barbarous is the destruction, and so distant, both in time and space, do the splendours of that once radiant city already seem.

There is not a single human being stirring: the only signs of life are garments hanging limply from a clothes line (Part 3), and a few disconsolate white cows sheltering under trees from the blistering midday sun (Parts 5, 6). The devastation, large-scale and brutal, has forced the population to flee in terror.

Just a few weeks before this scene was shot, William Howard Russell, London correspondent of *The Times*, surveying Lucknow for the first time from the terrace of the Dilkusha, described the city in these terms:

'A vision indeed! A vision of palaces, minars, domes azure and golden, cupolas, colonnades, long facades of fair perspective in pillar and column, terraced roofs – all rising up amid a calm, still ocean of the brightest verdure.

Look for miles and miles away, and still the ocean spreads, and the towers of the fairy city gleam in its midst. Spires of gold glitter in the sun. Turrets and gilded spheres shine like constellations. There is nothing mean or squalid to be seen.

There is a city more vast than Paris, as it seems, and more brilliant, lying before us. Is this a city in Oude? Is this the capital of a semi-barbarous race, erected by a corrupt, effete and degraded dynasty? I confess I felt inclined to rub my eyes again and again …

Not Rome, not Athens, not Constantinople, not any city I have ever seen, appears to me so striking and beautiful as this; and the more I gaze, the more its beauties grow upon me.'

Some days later, Russell recalled in his diary the desecration of the Qaisarbagh complex that he had witnessed:

'The scene of plunder was indescribable. The soldiers had broken open several of the store-rooms, and pitched the contents into the court, which was lumbered with cases, with embroidered clothes, gold drums, shawls, scarves, musical instruments, gorgeous standards, shields, spears, and a heap of things … Through these moved the men, wild with excitement, 'drunk with plunder'.

I had often heard the phrase but never seen the thing itself before. They smashed to pieces the fowling pieces and pistols to get at the gold mountings and the stones set in the stocks. They burned in a fire brocades and embroidered shawls for the sake of the gold and silver. China, glass and jade they smashed to pieces in pure wantonness; pictures they ripped up, or tossed on the flames; furniture shared the same fate …

Done up beyond expression, I threw myself on a charpoy, and for an hour slept a sleep of dreams almost as bad as the realities I had just witnessed.' [1]

Eighteen years later, accompanying the Prince of Wales, Albert Edward, on his tour of India, William Howard Russell confided to his diary:

'January 6, 1876

Lucknow has been fairly 'improved' off the face of the earth.

Hundreds of acres once occupied by houses have been turned into market gardens. Swarded parks, vistas, rides and drives, far prettier than those of the Bois de Boulogne, spread out where once were streets, bazaars, palaces.

They are like oceans beneath which thousands of wrecks lie buried…' [2]

Fig. 48: Felice Beato, The Bara Imambara and environs, eight albumen prints, 1858.

Part 1: Jama Masjid and Husainabad Imambara

Part 2: Daulat Khana

Part 3: Rumi Darwaza

Part 4: Entrance to the Bara Imambara and Aurangzeb Mosque

Part 5: *Tripolia* and Panch Mahalla Gateway

Part 6: Macchi Bhawan

Part 7: Entrance to the Ba'oli and Bara Imambara

Part 8: Bara Imambara and minaret of the Asafi Mosque

Chapter Two

MONUMENTAL GRIEF:
THE BARA IMAMBARA

Peter Chelkowski

Lucknow exists but to mourn Husain.
Rightly it can be called the home of Husain.
                    Dilgir

The Bara Imambara at Lucknow, also known as the Great Imambara or the Asafi Imambara, is the world's largest complex of buildings devoted to the rituals and cult of Imam Husain. It has stood proudly for more than two centuries, a testament to the design and structural ingenuity of its builders. In terms of grandeur it can be compared only with the monumental Mughal tombs. Before examining the building of this great edifice, however, we will take a brief look at the source and history of Shia rituals in order to throw some light on the importance and function of imambaras.

In the year 61 of the Muslim calendar (AD 680), a battle took place at Karbala, a barren desert in what is now Iraq. It was there that the rituals and myths surrounding Imam Husain originated. Husain – the champion of the Shia cause, the son of Ali and the grandson of the Prophet Muhammad –

was on his way to join his fellow Shia partisans in the city of Kufa when he was ambushed in the desert. Along with his entire family and (according to tradition) a group of seventy-two male followers, Husain was massacred by the numerically superior forces of the caliph Yazid, the leader of the Sunni Muslims. The battle took place on the day of Ashura, the tenth day of the month of Muharram. This tragedy has assumed immense historical, spiritual and cultural significance for the Shias, who view it as the greatest suffering and sacrifice in history. It has transcended time and space to acquire importance of cosmic magnitude.

Mourning Rituals

The timeless quality of this sacrificial event has allowed the Shias continually to measure themselves against the principles and example of Husain. To this day, they strive to combat

Fig. 49: Shepherd & Robertson, Bara Imambara Gateway, albumen print (detail), c. 1862.

mode in which they deliver their lines. The protagonists sing their parts in the classical Persian styles (*dastgah*), while the antagonists speak theirs. All parts, whether sung or spoken, are in rhymed verse.[11]

Taziya is a noun derived from the Arabic verb *azza*, which means 'to mourn, to condole, to express one's sympathy'. In Iran, as we have seen, the emotions of the *taziya* are expressed through dramatic Shia Muslim passion plays. In India, these same feelings of lamentation are demonstrated in artistic renditions of Husain's tomb. In fact, although most of the stationary and ambulatory rituals in India seem almost identical to those in Iran, there are major differences.

The Ritual in India

In India, the Shia mourning period lasts eight days longer than that in Iran. It stretches from the first of Muharram, through the following month of Safar and into the first octave of Rabi-ul-Awwal. On the eighth day of Rabi-ul-Awwal, the eleventh Imam, Hasan Askari, was martyred. In India, the self-mortification – called *matam* – is somewhat more severe, as the flagellants attach razor blades to their chains in order to lacerate their backs. The *alams* in India are somewhat smaller than those found in Iran. The elephants that march in Indian processions are definitely not found in Iran, and the Iranians do not walk barefoot on burning coals as the Indians do. The stationary rituals, commonly called *majalis* (plural form of the word *majlis*, meaning assembly or gathering), follow the Iranian tradition of reciting or chanting Husain's saga to and by an assembly of mourners. Ten chapters of *Rauzat al-shuhada*, known as *Dah Majlis*, had already appeared in India by the end of the sixteenth century. By the end of the seventeenth century the first translation into Deccani poetry had appeared. *Dah Majlis* appeared in Urdu translation in 1791/92. Like the *rauza-khans* in Iran, the men who stage the *majalis* in India manipulate the mood and the emotions of the audience through voice modulation, chanting, crying and gesturing. According to Professor S. A. A. Rizvi, 'The mourning assemblies re-affirm the conviction that truth and justice prevail and the forces of evil and injustice do not survive.'[12]

There are, however, even more fundamental differences between the Shia mourning observances of India and Iran. These are dictated by the great distance of India from Karbala. Every Shia Muslim longs to go on pilgrimage (*ziyarat*) to the tomb of Husain. A great number would like to be buried near his tomb. For centuries, caravans have conveyed the bodies of the dead from Iran to Karbala to be buried there. In places far from Karbala, such as India, however, pilgrimages were prohibitive for reasons of geography, economics and politics. Even with the modern possibilities of refrigeration, the transportation of the dead from India to Karbala is an almost impossible proposition. Thus, since India could not be taken to Karbala, the Shias devised a way to bring Karbala to India: earth was brought from Karbala to be sprinkled over the local burial ground. Once 'Karbala' was there, the next logical step was to bring the mausoleum of Husain to India as well. In this fashion, the *taziya* of India was conceived.

The *Taziya*

The re-creation of Husain's tomb according to the sensibilities and inspiration of individual artists is seen as an act of piety and as homage to Husain. If these fabrications have any correspondence to reality, it is more in their resemblance to the architecture of Indian mosques than to their similarity to Husain's actual mausoleum. An Indian *taziya* can be tiny or it can be a gigantic 40-foot high installation of bamboo, covered with papier mâché, tinsel, silk and jewellery. Some *taziya* require lavish expenditure and months of construction. Whether they are small or big, humble or rich, all *taziya* are believed to possess healing power.

Thousands of *taziya* of various shapes and sizes are built every year and are carried in processions during the months of mourning. They are displayed in private and public imambaras and finally buried in the local karbalas (Shia cemeteries). In a way, a *taziya* is a symbolic cenotaph, but at the same time it is a ritual bier on which Husain's body is carried for burial. So in India the participation in the procession with the *taziya* is at once a pilgrimage to Husain's tomb and a re-enactment of his funeral.

Hair-raising though this may be to pious Muslims, it is a fact of cultural history that Hindu rituals such as the Durga Puja and the festival of Jagannath had a significant influence on the Indian *taziya* rituals. The pavilion of the goddess Durga, called the *pandal*, and the conveyance of Jagannath, the *rath* (some 40 feet high), are carried or drawn along a processional route for the people's *darshan*. During *darshan*, the Hindu faithful view these two structures with devotion and awe and believe they receive healing and blessing from the *pandal* and the *rath*. This corresponds to the sentiments of the participants and spectators in a *taziya* procession. In both cases, after the procession is concluded, the revered structures are restored to the elements – water and earth.[13]

Shakeel Hossain calls the *taziya* 'the ephemeral transient' architecture.[14] After it is built, it is displayed for a very short time and then carried in procession either to be buried at the local karbala or to be immersed in water (if there is a river, a lake or the sea nearby); this is no doubt a Hindu influence. In addition to the *taziya* there is a more permanent structure representing Husain's tomb, called a *zarih*. For some, a *zarih* is a railing that fences or encases a tomb. There is a general disagreement in literature as to what constitutes a ritual *zarih*. If a *taziya* is a ritual mausoleum of Husain, the *zarih* is a ritual cenotaph of Husain. According to some, the *zarih* has a dome and the *taziya* does not have one. But there is no consistency to this rule. I myself have seen many *taziyas* with domes. An account of a nineteenth-century resident of Lucknow, Mrs Meer Hassan Ali, highlights this confusion. She describes a structure made of coloured glass and bronze moulding and manufactured in England in the early nineteenth century as a *taziya* rather than a *zarih*: '... I have seen some beautifully wrought in silver filigree. The handsomest of the kind to my taste is in the possession of his Majesty the King of Oude composed of green glass, with brass mouldings manufactured in England. All these expensive Tazias are fixtures.'[15]

Despite uncertainty as to the exact distinction between *taziya* and *zarih*, popular lore has it that Timur (Tamerlane, 1336–1405) brought the tradition of *taziya* to India. 'Consequent upon the consolidation of Mughal supremacy in India, it became widely known that King Timor was the first person to have made such a model [Tazia] of Imam Husain's tomb.'[16] The logical assumption is that Timur would have preferred to have a *zarih* accompany him rather than an ephemeral *taziya*. But Timur's zealous descendants may have purposely 'rearranged' some historical facts. As S. A. A. Rizvi writes: 'In the 18th and 19th centuries, the Mughal princes who embraced Shi'sm spread the myth that their ancestor Timur had been a Shia and had introduced *taziyas* into India. [But] no literary evidence supports this.'[17] Additional dissimilarities between *taziyas* and *zarihs* are found in their burial methods. A *zarih* is not buried; only its extraneous decorations, such as flower garlands, are interred. The *zarih* itself is returned to the imambara. A *taziya* is built anew every year; a *zarih* is re-used again and again – only its decorations are new.

Another factor contributing to the differences between the Indian and Iranian ritual observances is the disparity in the ethno-religious composition of both countries. Iran is a relatively homogeneous society, with 90% of the population being Twelver Shias. (The Twelver Shias – who view the twelve imams as the true successors to Muhammad – are the largest and the strongest of the various Shia groups, and are the focus of the discussion in this chapter.) India, by contrast, is a veritable ethnic and religious mosaic: the Shias of India are like small islands in an ocean of Hinduism and Sunni Islam. Climate also plays a role in how rituals are performed. Iran enjoys hospitable, continental dry weather, while in India the climate is hot, humid and dependent on the vagaries of monsoon. From the sixteenth century onwards, we witness in India the need for permanent ritual-oriented buildings which could serve as loci for various stationary rituals, as the point of departure and arrival for processions, and as a repository for the many symbolic objects used in processions, such as *taziyas*, *zarihs* and *alams*.

The Architecture of Mourning

It is a fallacy to think, as do many western and Indian scholars, that the origin of the buildings devoted to the Twelver Shia rituals is to be found in Iran. Such edifices, called in Iran *Husainiya* or *takiya*, were not developed there until the late eighteenth century. In India, however, this type of architecture can be traced to the last quarter of the sixteenth century. In southern India these buildings are called *ashurkhanas*, and in northern India imambaras, but they are also known as *azakhanas*, *Husainiyas* and *taziyakhanas*. *Ashurkhana* means the house of Ashura (the tenth day of Muharram). As David Pinault explains:

'The ashurkhana has a number of functions. It serves as an assembly place where majalis are held during Muharram and jeshans or festive assemblies are held during other seasons of the year; it is used as a storehouse for the alams (copies of battle-standards or banners borne by the martyrs of Karbala) and the tazias that are carried in the Muharram processions.'[18]

The establishment of Shia kingdoms in the Deccan region of south-central India precipitated the movement of a great number of Persians into this area. When the architectural forerunners of the imambaras, the *ashurkhanas*, were built in the Deccan, their primary function was to house the *alams*. The other function of *ashurkhanas* in the Deccan has been as loci for the mourning *majalis*. However, these *ashurkhanas* were typically of much smaller size in comparison with the public imambaras of Lucknow. The oldest *ashurkhana* seems to be the Badshahi Ashurkhana, which was constructed in the year 1596 in Hyderabad, the capital of the Golconda kingdom, almost two hundred years before the Bara Imambara at Lucknow.

Nawab Asaf-ud-daula's architectural achievements at Lucknow were so splendid that they stood as an ambitious challenge to the later nawabs and kings that followed him. Among all his monuments, the imambara was the most magnificent. It was an unmistakable statement of independence from Delhi. There is no doubt that the proliferation of imambaras – both public and private – in Lucknow helped to make it the centre of Shi'ism in northern India. The imambaras in Awadh were built on a grander scale than those of Hyderabad, and played a slightly different role. They were primarily places of display for *taziyas* and permanent houses for *zarihs*.

As for a comparison of the imambaras of Lucknow with the Muharram-related edifices of Iran – the *takiya* and *Husainiya* – it is evident that the Persian structures never achieved the same size or architectural splendour as their counterparts in Awadh. A possible exception is the Royal Muharram Theatre, built in Tehran by Nasr al-din Shah in the 1870s. Known as the Takiya Dowlat, the theatre was praised by many foreign visitors to Iran in the last quarter of the nineteenth century. However, despite its sumptuousness, which many believed to be based on the Royal Albert Hall in London, the Takiya Dowlat was poorly constructed in haste and had to be pulled down after World War II.

In the eighteenth century, the great centralized Islamic empires of Ottoman Turkey, Safavid Iran and Mughal India started to unravel. Concurrently with the beginning of this decentralization in India, though unrelated to it, the religious orientation of the new emperor skewed from orthodox Sunnism towards Twelver Shi'ism. After the death of the Mughal emperor Aurangzeb in 1707, his successor, Bahadur Shah, was notably sympathetic towards Twelver Shi'ism. In these circumstances, Mir Muhammed Amin Nishapuri from Khorasan in north-eastern Persia established himself at the royal court in Delhi. Thanks to his administrative abilities and courtly talents, he soon received the title of Saadat Khan Bahadur and was made governor of Agra. In September of 1722, Nishapuri's spectacular career was crowned with his appointment as governor of Awadh. This appointment was the beginning of the independent hereditary governorship, and later kingship, of Awadh, which lasted for 136 years.

The Nishapuri family had a long tradition of propagating Twelver Shi'ism. Though their house was a bastion for the promotion of Persian culture, the Nishapuris were even more strongly committed to spreading their faith. Their ancestors were brought to Nishapur by Shah Isma'il Safavid (1501–1524), from Najaf, the centre of Shia learning, in order to spread Twelver Shi'ism in Persia. There is a very interesting parallel between the nawabi house of Awadh and the later Qajar dynasty in Persia. Both were very concerned with Shia rituals and popular beliefs and incorporated them into state functions. However, on the Indian subcontinent, both Sunnis and Hindus took part in Muharram observances, with participation in Awadh being greater than anywhere else.

The liberal ethno-religious climate of India has been conducive for both non-Shia Muslims and Hindus to participate actively in Husain rituals. Sadiq Naqvi writes:

'Ashurkhana is a meeting place of people of all religions and castes who forget their differences. It is only here that one, whether Muslim or Hindu, Shi'a or Sunni could participate in the proceedings in his own way and according to his own belief … the Ashurkhana thus serves as a platform for the people of diversified societies to meet in a brotherly atmosphere.'[19]

This is further underlined by Dr M. Zore, who notes that in *Ashurkhana* 'the differences between the ruler and the ruled and the differences of culture, religion, and caste were forgotten'.[20]

The Bara Imambara of Lucknow

Imambaras can be public or private constructions; often they are no more than a room, or even just a small shrine on the wall, in a private house. In every instance, however, they are places of honour reserved to house the *taziya*. As Neeta Das explains:

'To perpetuate the memories of Karbala, Imambaras have taken an important part in a Shia's life and even the poorest Shia has a place of honour set aside for the "Tazia," even if it is a small niche in the wall. Families better off have allocated rooms for this purpose with a raised platform, the "shah nashin," for keeping the Tazia which remains screened off when not in use, and the room is used for sitting at other times of the year. It is considered an act of charity by the affluent Shias to make Imambaras and organize the Muharram celebrations. The residential Imambaras are used mostly by the Muslim ladies in 'Purdah' whereas the public Imambaras are for the male members of the family.'[21]

J. R. I. Cole notes that 'the imambarahs made statements not only of piety, but also of wealth, power, and status'.[22]

The construction of the Bara Imambara of Lucknow (fig. 48), the crowning achievement of imambara architecture, occurred while the establishment of its counterpart in Iran, the *takiya*, was still in its infancy. The architect of the imambara, Kifayutaullah (or Kifayutollah), is believed to have been Persian, but his creation has no antecedents in Iran. Nawab Asaf-ud-daula, who commissioned the imambara, was a great builder with ambition to make his new capital at Lucknow an architectural wonder. Since he was very pious he wanted to erect next to his palace, Macchi Bhawan, an exemplary building devoted to the Shia observances. The building would act both as a place for the stationary rituals, the *majalis*, and a gallery for the representational tombs of Husain, the *taziyas* and *zarihs*. As Rosie Llewellyn-Jones explains:

'These portable shrines (*taziya*), representing the graves of Husain and Hasan, are often extremely elaborate and are housed for a year in imambaras before they are taken through the streets to be ceremoniously buried. The *taziyas* are invested with an immense feeling of sacredness and the fact that they must be housed in a suitably solemn and grand building led to the development of the imambaras which reached its ultimate expression in Lucknow and especially in the Great Imambara built by Asaf-ud-daula in 1784, which, at one time, contained the largest vaulted hall in the world.'[23]

The building of this immense imambara, which took place in 1784–91, was not a simple act of Twelver Shia devotion:

the nawab was making a political statement. The topograph-ical limitations of the terrain west of the Macchi Bhawan – which comprises a ravine steeply rising to a hill – were not conducive to the building of a huge architectural complex. But Asaf-ud-daula overcame these obstacles in order to link the palace with the Twelver Shia mosque and imambara. Thus, not only the local Hindu and Sunni Muslim popula-tion but also the government in Delhi had to recognize the nawab's growing power.

European visitors to the site were awed by its magnificence. William Knighton described its architectural layout:

'The royal Emanbarra stands near the "Constantinople gate" of Lucknow [the Rumi Darwaza] – a gate built on the model of that which gave to the court of the sultan the title of "the Sublime Porte". Both structures, the gate and the Emanbarra, are elegant and harmonize well with each other. Two square courts extend in front of the building of the Emanbarra, beautifully decorated with rich tessellated pave-ments. The inner of these courts is raised several feet above the level of the outer. The Emanbarra belongs to that style of architecture aptly called by Bishop Heber "the oriental Gothic".'[24]

To some it appeared so extraordinary that it might almost have been fashioned by fantastical means. Emma Roberts wrote in 1837:

'Without entering further into dry descriptive details, it may be sufficient to say, that in no place in India can there be a more vivid realization of visions conjured up by a perusal of the splendid fictions of the *Arabian Nights*. Those who have visited the Kremlin have pronounced that far-famed edifice to be inferior to the Imambara.'[25]

George Annesley, later Viscount Valentia, who had the opportunity of travelling all over India, visited the Great Imambara in 1803 and recorded his impressions:

'The Rumi Derwazah was built after, [it] was supposed, one of the gates of Constantinople, though it is of that light,

elegant, but fantastic architecture which has some little resemblance to the Gothic and Morisco, but none to the Grecian. The Imaumbarah, the mosque attached to it, and the gateways that lead to it, are beautiful specimens of this architecture. From the brilliant white of the composition, and the minute delicacy of the workmanship, an enthusiast might suppose that Genii had been the artificers.'[26]

Until the final clearance of the Macchi Bhawan site in the late nineteenth century, the imambara was closely linked to the former palace. Today, the complex consists of the imam-bara itself (fig. 59), fronted by three successive courtyards (fig. 57), the ceremonial Rumi Darwaza (figs. 52 & 54), the Asafi Mosque (fig. 69) and the Ba'oli (a step well with sub-terranean apartments used during heatwaves). The imam-bara is built on two axes, north–south (the principal axis) and east–west. A forecourt once existed on the east–west axis; today this is a road open to traffic. On the western end of this court is the ornamental Rumi Darwaza. There has been a lot of speculation as to the meaning of the name 'Rumi'. I believe that 'Rum' here indicates not only Byzan-tium (Rum in Arabic means the Eastern Roman Empire) but the Roman Empire as well, and that the Rumi Darwaza is the equivalent of a Roman triumphal arch. On the eastern side of this forecourt there was once a gate which, from a design standpoint, corresponded to the inner façade of the Rumi Darwaza (fig. 48, part 5). It was not an exact copy, but it contained similarities. This eastern gateway was destroyed by the British shortly after 1858, along with part of the Macchi Bhawan palace. Both gates were equidistant from the first gate on the north–south axis, which is today the main gate to the imambara complex. The entire area between the Rumi and eastern gates was enclosed by a wall; in this fashion the first courtyard was secure. Opposite the main gateway there was a facsimile or *jawab* gate with foli-ated arches (figs. 53 & 56). This gate did not lead anywhere; it was built to provide symmetry with the first courtyard.

The second courtyard is rectangular and measures some 230 x 300 feet. On the southern side of this courtyard is a flight of nineteen steps leading to the triple-arched interior gate (figs. 55 & 70); this is similar in design to the main gate but with some minor differences. The interior gate is considered to be the most elegant of all the portals in the imambara complex thanks to its position, which allows it to be viewed from the wide-open vista of the third courtyard. The third courtyard is 9 feet higher than the second. Originally, as indicated in mid-nineteenth-century photographs, there were no steps connecting the two courtyards but merely a dirt incline leading to the interior gate. This allowed the animals taking part in ritual processions to be led into the third courtyard if necessary. Today, animals can enter only the first and second courtyards.

The third and main courtyard is almost one-and-a-half times as long as the second, and fronts the imambara building. Its appearance today differs markedly from when it was laid out, primarily because of the vast cascade of steps that now spills into the western portion of the courtyard from the mosque. Photographs from the 1860s and early 1870s show that the ground floor of the mosque originally contained a series of arched cells where pilgrims could rest and sleep. It seems that the British blocked these up, raised a mound in front of the mosque and built the steps up it for security reasons, in order to prevent future adversaries from hiding in the cells. The mosque stood on its own axis, as it was necessary for it to face south-west towards Mecca (fig. 58). With the mosque placed in this spot, the entire complex became very 'un-Indian' since its placement broke the symmetry so dear to Indian and, particularly, Muslim Indian architecture. This unusual placement was due to the limitations of the site's topography – otherwise, the whole complex would no doubt have been aligned with Mecca. Nevertheless, the complex does exude a feeling of unity. It is apparent that the architect thought out even the smallest details. For example, the third courtyard widens imperceptibly as it spreads south; thus a viewer standing in the interior gate has a 'telescopic' view, which creates the impression that the width of the courtyard at the north is equal to the width at its southern end. In addition, the north–south axis running from the imambara building to the main gate is slightly skewed, so that direct sunlight will not fall upon the northern façade of the imambara building itself – thus keeping this area perpetually cool.

The hill upon which the complex stands slopes gently to the north – towards the River Gomti – and steeply towards the west and the ravine, at the bottom of which is a rivulet. The slope creates a natural drainage pattern, which is especially helpful during the monsoon season. The imambara is constructed upon a brick platform (fig. 65). The two main courtyards were formed by cutting into the hillside, the eastern portion of which became a decorative retaining wall with eighty-eight arches on two levels (Macchi Bhawan palace was more than ten feet above the third courtyard). Also on the eastern side of the third court is a small gate that leads to the Ba'oli. This nawabi well was sunk deep enough to correspond to the level of the Gomti, which meanders north of the imambara from the north-west to the south-east.

At the end of the third courtyard, eighteen steps (they are original to the site) lead to the imambara's massive terrace, which measures 71 x 260 feet. The grandiose scale reflects the fact that the complex was built as a response to the Mughal monumental architecture. Since the word 'imambara' means 'dwelling place of the Imam', it seems only right and proper that the approach should be through a series of progressively elevated courtyards and flights of steps, ending – as is the case at Lucknow – in the imambara itself. A complex so designed allows the faithful to come and pray as if they were making a symbolic pilgrimage to the real tomb in Karbala.

The Bara Imambara is built entirely of brick covered with stucco. (Sandstone and marble, the materials used for Mughal tombs, were not available in this region.). A large number of highly talented masons, able to lay bricks and apply stucco with equal skill, were active in the area at this time. Small, hard *lakhori* bricks, measuring 3/4 x 3 7/8 x 5 7/8 inches, were used with mortar to lend elasticity to the walls, and the stucco was applied in such a way that it resembled marble. The stucco was durable and possessed an extraordinary sheen. As John Pemble points out:

'The Lucknow stucco, made from the calcareous deposits of ancient lake beds, gave an effect of great chasteness when not covered with surface distemper, and its toughness was fully attested in 1858, when the plastered walls of [a] building called Sikandarbagh proved indestructible by nine-pound cannon shot and yielded to the British eighteen-pounders only after more than an hour's bombardment.'[27]

The interior of the imambara was also resplendent with the brilliance of the local stucco. Using recovered lime or shells from dried-up lakes, the masons were able to produce stucco that shone more brilliantly than the marble tombs of the Mughals.

Though Imam Husain is the focal point of the entire complex, originally there were also fourteen cenotaphs of pure silver on display representing the 'fourteen sinless'. One was for the Prophet, another for his daughter Fatimah, and the remaining twelve for the twelve Imams. Abdu'l Wahhab Qazvini, a visitor to the imambara in the nineteenth century, observed that 'In the Great Imambarah stood fourteen tombs of pure silver, one for each of the Twelve Imams, the Prophet, and Fatimah.'[28] An important point should be made about the Twelfth Imam, however. According to Shia Muslim history and belief, the first eleven Imams died and were buried, but the twelfth did not die; rather, he went into concealment by occultation (in hiding) and was removed from human view. It is believed that he will return as Mahdi, or the Messiah. Therefore, this 'tomb' of his is extraneous.

The remaining grave is the 'real' tomb of the founder of the complex, who was buried within as a 'fringe benefit', receiving merit vicariously through the prayers offered to Imam Husain. Viscount Valentia further described the tomb of Nawab Asaf-ud-daula in his memoir:

'The Imaumbarah is certainly the most beautiful building I have seen in India; it was erected by the late Nawaub, for the double purpose of celebrating this festival [Muharram], and of serving as a burial place for himself. It consists of three very long and finely proportioned apartments, running parallel to each other: in the middle is his tomb, level with the ground. The centre is earth covered with a scanty herbage, and surrounded with a broad margin of white marble, in which sentences from the Koran are inlayed in black. At one end lies the sword, turban, etc. which he had on when he died. Over it is a rich canopy supported by four pillars, covered with a cloth of gold, now in decay. Unfortunately, it was necessary to place his tomb diagonally, that he might lie in a proper Mahomedan position respecting Mecca; and, consequently, instead of an ornament, it is an unsightly object.'[29]

Other observers have also found the position of the nawab's tomb to be jarring, and some have speculated that the imambara was not originally designed to be his resting place because the tomb does not follow the axis of the building. But as I have stressed earlier, this has to do with the topography of the site on which the imambara was built. It was impossible to have the entire complex oriented towards Mecca because of its necessary proximity to Macchi Bhawan palace. Therefore, only those elements mandated by Islamic law to face Mecca – the mosque and the tomb of the founder – were aligned in that direction.

The imambara is divided into nine chambers (fig. 62). The whole structure is intended to showcase the middle hall, which is 163 feet long and 53 feet wide. In the middle of this hall is the tomb of Nawab Asaf-ud-daula. It uses neither pillars nor crossbeams for support, and when it was completed, in 1791, this space was considered to be the largest vaulted hall in the world. Just before the roof starts its curve into the barrel vaults, at a height of 49½ feet, one notices a gallery running around the periphery of the space. This gallery, enclosed by stone grilled balustrades, or *jalis*, was reserved as the place for the women of the royal court to watch the ritual proceedings – they could 'see', but were 'unseen'.

The central chamber is flanked by northern and southern galleries, which are the same length as the central hall but half of its width. The southern gallery is raised three feet higher than the central hall. This section of the edifice was elevated in order better to display the cenotaphs, which rested between the foliated arches that are found throughout the entire complex (entering the imambara through the Rumi Gate, one is already confronted by the foliated arch).

The nine large and four small arches on the northern façade of the imambara building are in this style, as are the arches that connect the nine interior chambers to one another.

The central hall, popularly known as the 'Persian' Hall, is connected on its eastern end to the 'Chinese' Hall (the ceiling stucco decoration of which is reminiscent of Chinese decorative art (fig. 63) and on its western end to the 'Indian' Hall (fig. 64). The eastern and western chambers are each constructed on a square floor plan, which opens to an octagonal space crowned by a dome. These domes are visible only from the interior of the imambara. If it were not for the curving apex of the domes, these two chambers – which measure 53½ feet at their length, height and apex respectively – would be perfect cubes. The ceiling in all three halls is supported by repeated squinches of very intricate and beautiful design. Rising from ground level are four levels of small-arched corridors creating a so-called labyrinth, which runs along the length and width of the imambara. This maze of arches is listed in most tourist guidebooks as the major architectural attraction in Lucknow. The purpose of this labyrinth is to support and buttress the roof. Its enduring utility and grace remain the best testaments to the ingenuity of the architect: although the building has stood for more than two hundred years, no visible structural damage has ever been noted.[30]

While these architectural accomplishments are rightly singled out by historians and local guides, nineteenth-century visitors to the interior of the imambara were repeatedly awed more by its illumination scheme than by its structural wonders. The profusion and brilliance of light surrounded and dazzled the viewer. Mrs Meer Hassan Ali wrote:

'On the walls of the Emaum-baarah, mirrors and looking-glasses are fixed in suitable situations to give effect to the brilliant display of light from the magnificent chandeliers suspended from the cupola and cornices. The nobles and the wealthy are excited with a desire to emulate each other in the splendour of their display on these occasions.'[31]

Rosie Llewellyn-Jones also notes the effect of the lighting on visitors:

'But the most striking feature (for Europeans at any rate) is the absolute profusion inside the imambara of chandeliers of all shapes and sizes and the huge stands for lamps and candles, often five feet or more in height, and made from highly decorated china, coloured glass and metals. The effect when all the chandeliers and stands are lit is dazzling, especially in the cool and dark halls of the imambara … '[32]

The magnificence of the Great Imambara at Lucknow made it a magnet for European tourists, but it also served its intended visitors by making the Husain rituals attractive to all levels of the Shia population. This was already evident two or three years after it was built. S. A. A. Rizvi cites in his work an account of Nawab Asaf-ud-daula's activities during the Muharram of 1794–95, as related in the court akhbar (news bulletin) now in the possession of the Royal Asiatic Society in London. He explains:

'… the Asafiyya, or Bara Imambarah, was the centre of the mourning ceremonies organized by the Nawab. His visits to the imambarahs belonging to the begums, the dignitaries at court, and the poor citizens, had made the ashura mourning rituals popular with all sections of the [Lucknow] society.'[33]

Despite the vicissitudes of history, the Great Imambara has endured. It has survived foreign military occupation and desecration, and the destruction of the royal palace, which was an organic part of the complex to the east. It has outlasted the eastern gate, which once led to the first outer court, and the wall which demarcated the Asafi Mosque from the third courtyard. Today the imambara accommodates a vibrant community of the faithful as well as an ever growing number of tourists, both Indian and international, who gather at the site in awe, wonder and appreciation.

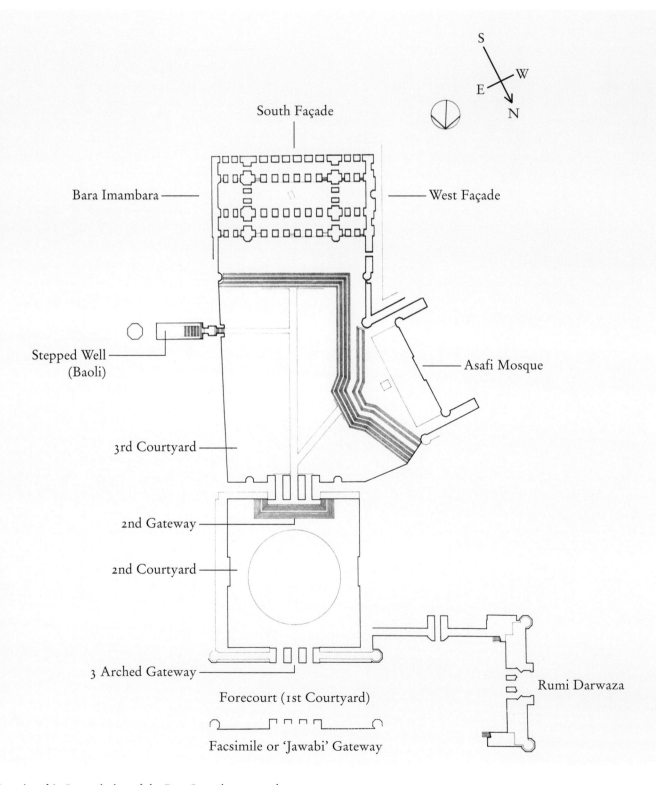

S
W
E
N

South Façade

Bara Imambara

West Façade

Stepped Well
(Baoli)

Asafi Mosque

3rd Courtyard

2nd Gateway

2nd Courtyard

Rumi Darwaza

3 Arched Gateway

Forecourt (1st Courtyard)

Facsimile or 'Jawabi' Gateway

Fig. 50: W. Sypniewski, Ground plan of the Bara Imambara complex, 2001.

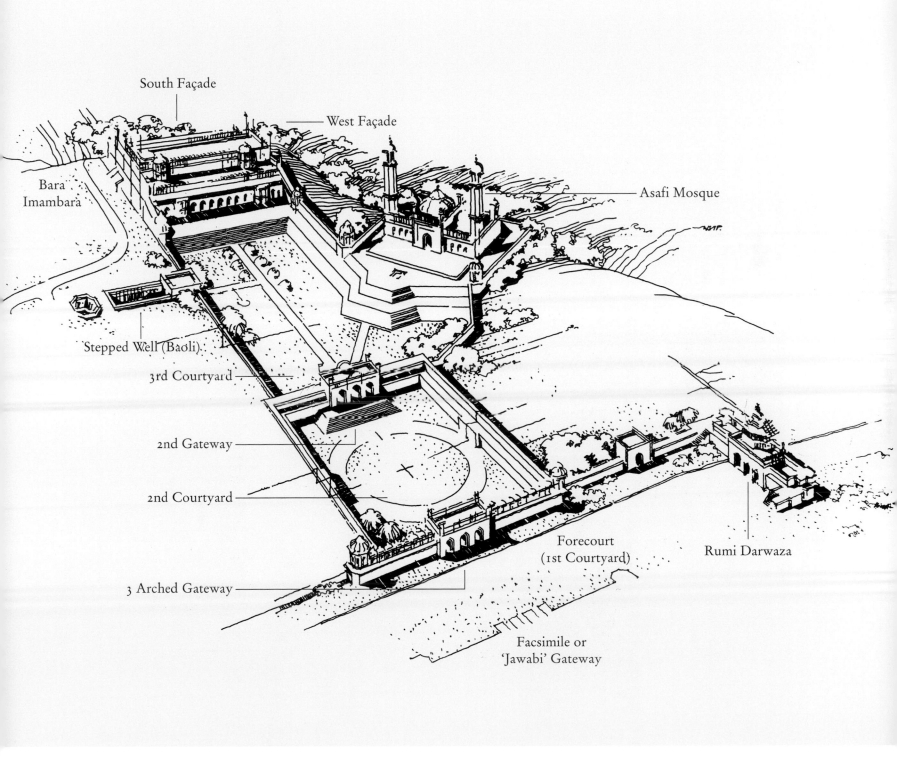

South Façade

West Façade

Bara
Imambara

Asafi Mosque

Stepped Well (Baoli)

3rd Courtyard

2nd Gateway

2nd Courtyard

Forecourt
(1st Courtyard)

Rumi Darwaza

3 Arched Gateway

Facsimile or
'Jawabi' Gateway

Fig. 51: W. Sypniewski, Bird's eye view of the Asafi Mosque and Bara Imambara complex, 2001.

Fig. 52: Unknown photographer, Rumi Darwaza, albumen print, 1890s.

Fig. 53: **Unknown photographer,** Rumi Darwaza, albumen print (detail of fig. 54), late 1860s.

Fig. 54: Unknown photographer, Rumi Darwaza and gateway of the Bara Imambara (left) with *jawab* (Facsimile Gateway) opposite, albumen print, late 1860s

Fig. 55: **The Phototype Company,** Gateway leading into the third courtyard, Bara Imambara complex, postcard, late 1890s.

Fig. 56: Unknown photographer, Detail of the *jawab* (Facsimile Gateway), Bara Imambara complex, gelatin silver print, 1912–13.

Fig. 57: Samuel Bourne, The Bara Imambara complex showing the second courtyard, Imambara and Asafi Mosque, albumen print,
December 1864–early 1865.

Fig. 58:
Clifton & Co.,
Asafi Mosque and Bara Imambara
viewed from the Rumi Darwaza,
gelatin silver print, c. 1900.

Fig. 59: Unknown photographer, The Bara Imambara under restoration, albumen print, 1870s.

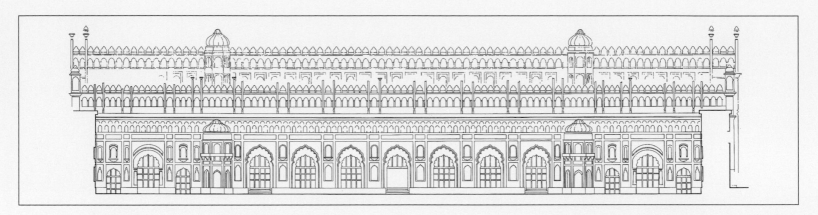

Fig. 60: W. Sypniewski, Front, or north façade, of the Bara Imambara, elevation, 2001.

Fig. 61: W. Sypniewski, Cutaway drawing showing the interior of the Bara Imambara, 2001.

Fig. 62: W. Sypniewski, East–west section through the Bara Imambara, 2001.

Fig. 63: W. Sypniewski, Section drawing of the 'Chinese Hall', 2001.

Fig. 64: W. Sypniewski, Section drawing of the 'Indian Hall', 2001.

Fig. 65: Felice Beato, The south-west façade of the Bara Imambara, albumen print, 1858.

Fig. 66: **Unknown photographer,** The rear, or south façade, of the Bara Imambara, albumen print, 1870s.

Fig. 67: Shepherd & Robertson, Asafi Mosque, west side, and Bara Imambara, south side, with the earth barricades from the Revolt of 1857, albumen print, c. 1862.

Fig. 68: G. W. Lawrie & Co., The rear, or south side, of the Bara Imambara, gelatin silver print, 1890s.

Fig. 69: Shepherd & Robertson, Asafi Mosque in the Bara Imambara complex, albumen print, c. 1862.

Fig. 70: Unknown photographer, Gateway leading from the third courtyard into the second courtyard, Bara Imambara, gelatin silver print, 1912–13.

been carved out of its broader setting. In this way the viewer is not distracted by features in the surrounding landscape that, while not extraneous, would draw his attention away from the underlying aesthetic principles on which the structure is based (fig. 71, detail).

The fundamental concept, that of symmetry – each significant form having its appropriate answer (*jawab*), or echo, or matching rhyme – is best exemplified in this exquisitely crafted architectural complex.

While the Great Imambara flaunts a flamboyant outer portal in the Rumi Darwaza, the Husainabad provides an elegant three-arched gateway that sets the mood for the visitor (fig. 72). Passing through this, the guest is startled by the presence of its visual 'echo' in the distance. He is then welcomed by the second entrance, which forms an integral part of the enclosure (fig. 73). This final gateway, in its turn, is mirrored by its twin.

Having ventured thus far, one is struck by the presence of the graceful tomb on the right (fig. 74), with its counterpart across the channel on the left (fig. 75). In the middle distance, the twinkling lights of the imambara beckon, and on approaching, one finds its delicate frontage shimmering in the waters of the channel below (fig. 81).

On a moonlit night, with the cool breeze rustling through the palm trees, the place exudes a seductive charm. Such frail beauty carries with it the unbearable poignancy of nights of mourning and lamentation in the month of Muharram.

It is with such subtle poetry that the views of Lucknow infused.

Fig. 71: Felice Beato, Two-part panorama of the Husainabad Imambara, the Daulat Khana to the left, the Rumi Darwaza and Bara Imambara to the right, albumen prints, 1858.

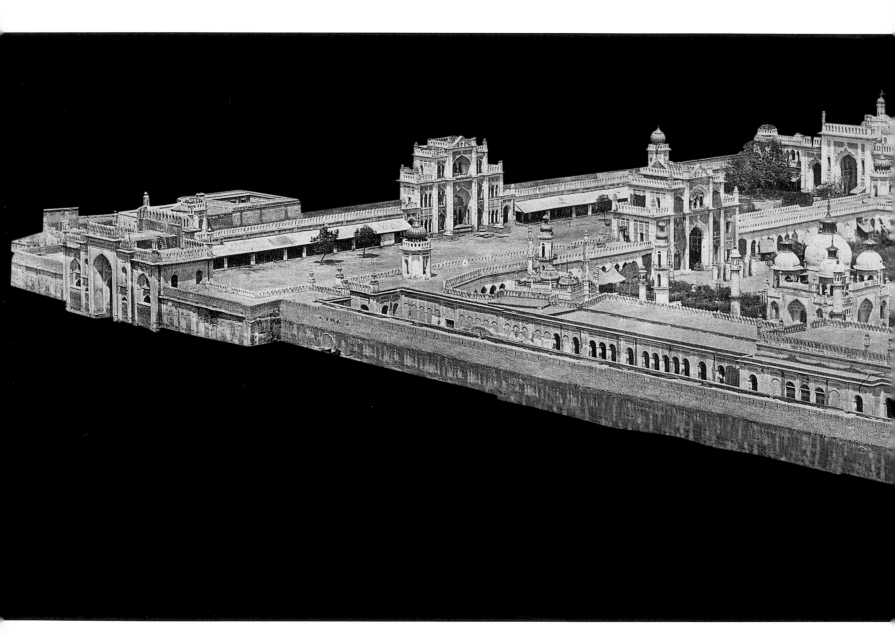

Fig. 71: **Felice Beato,** The Husainabad Imambara, albumen print, 1858 (detail).

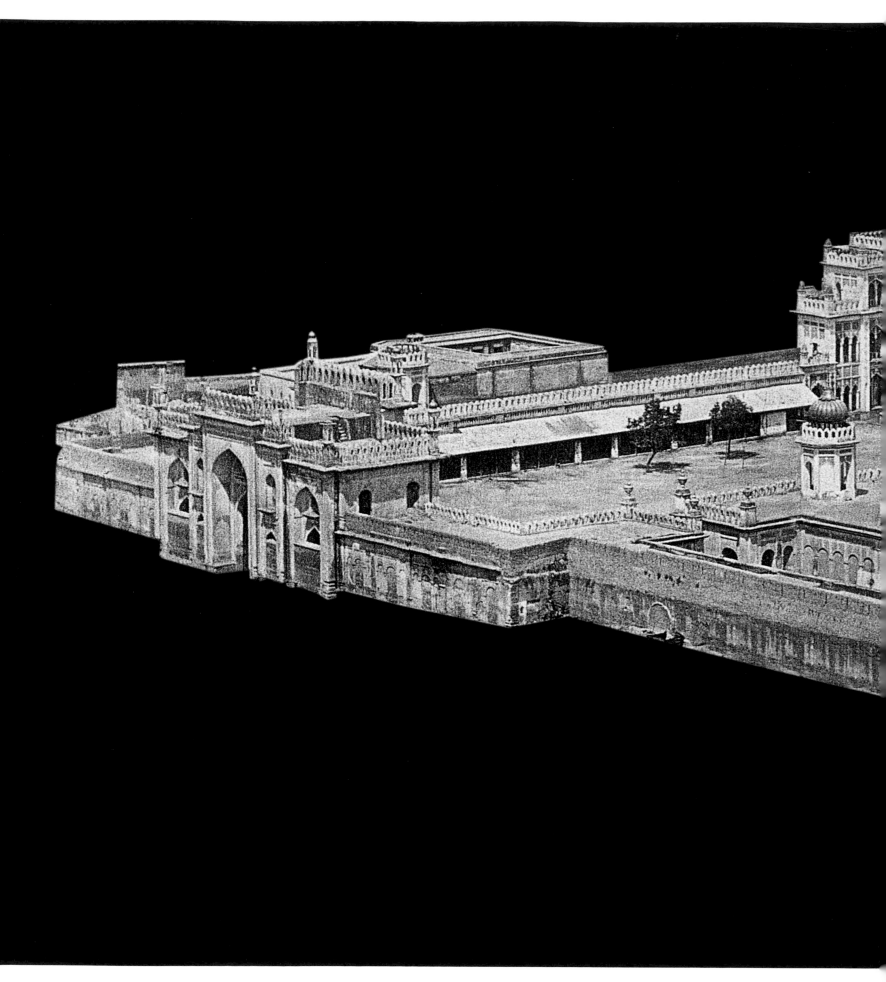

Fig. 71: **Felice Beato,** The Husainabad Imambara, albumen print, 1858 (detail, enlarged).

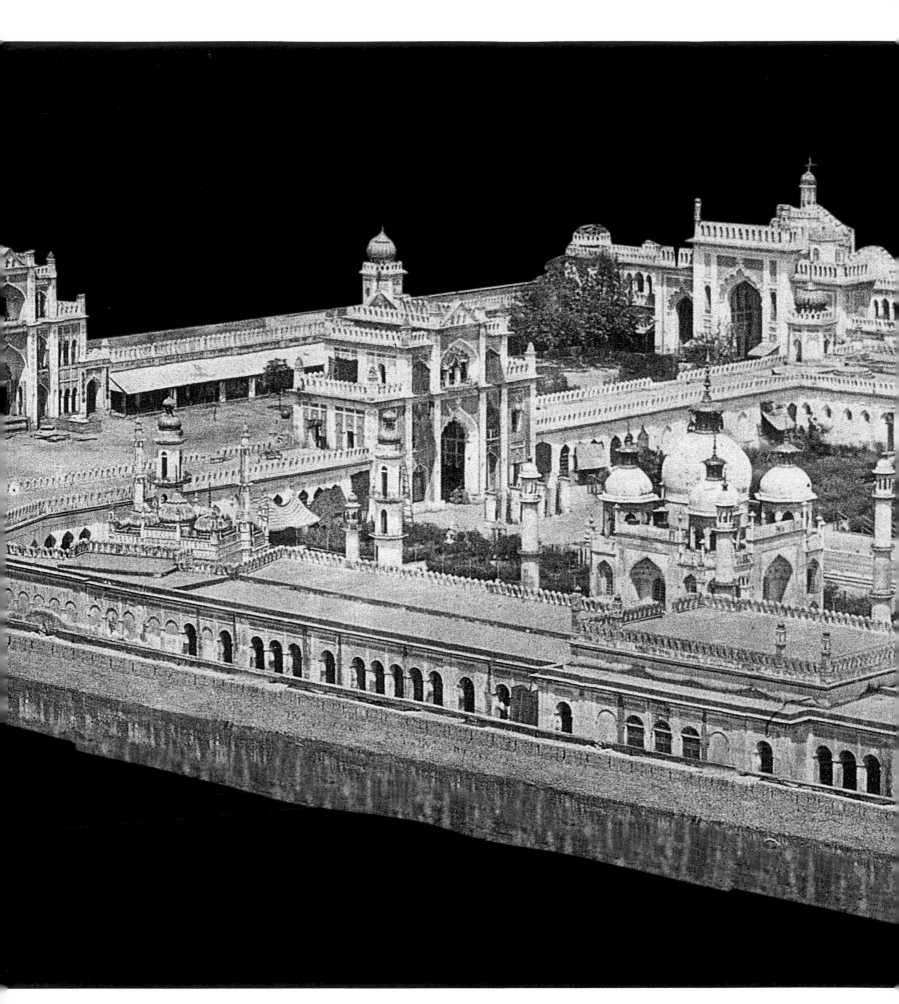

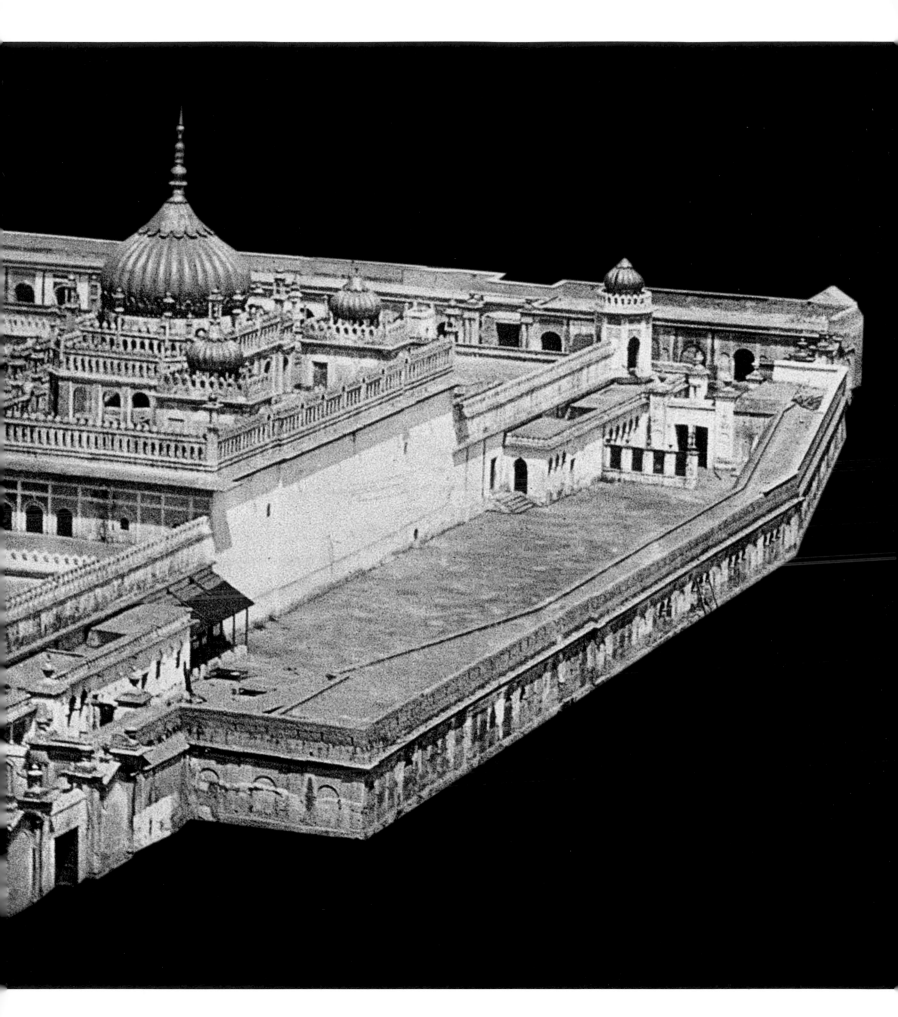

Fig. 72: John Edward Saché, Husainabad Bazaar Gateway, albumen print, c. 1867.

Fig. 73: Shepherd & Robertson, The Husainabad Imambara, Entrance Gateway seen from inside the complex, albumen print, c. 1862.

Fig. 74: Samuel Bourne, Tomb of Zinat Algiya and the Husainabad Mosque, albumen print, December 1864–early 1865.

Fig. 75: Frith's Series, *Jawab* opposite the Tomb of Zinat Algiya at the Husainabad Imambara, albumen print, late 1860s.

Fig. 76: John Edward Saché, Tomb of Zinat Algiya, with the mosque to the right, Husainabad Imambara, albumen print, C. 1867.

Fig. 77: Edmund David Lyon, *Jawab* facing the Tomb of Zinat Algiya at the Husainabad Imambara, albumen print, c. 1862.

Fig. 78: Unknown photographer, Husainabad Imambara and *jawab* facing the Tomb of Zinat Algiya on the left, postcard, late 1890s.

Fig. 79: John Edward Saché, Husainabad Imambara, with the Tomb of Zinat Algiya on the right, albumen print, c. 1867.

Fig. 80: Unknown photographer, Husainabad Imambara, View across the *talao*, albumen print, 1860s.

Fig. 81: **Unknown photographer,** Calligraphy on the façade of the Husainabad Imambara, albumen print (detail), late 1870s.

Fig. 82:
Unknown photographer,
Husainabad Imambara,
albumen print, 1870s.

Fig. 83: Unknown photographer, The Karbala Kazmain, salt print, c. 1856.

Fig. 84: The Phototype Company, Imambara Shah Najaf (Najaf-i-Ashraf), postcard, late 1890s.

Fig. 85: John Edward Saché, The Husainabad *talao* and Bazaar Gateway, with Sat Khande on the right and Jama Masjid in the distance, albumen print, c. 1867.

Fig. 86: G. W. Lawrie & Co., View across the *talao* towards the Husainabad Bazaar Gateway, with the Jama Masjid beyond, gelatin silver print, 1890s.

Fig. 87: Unknown photographer, Jama Masjid, postcard, c. 1912–13.

Fig. 88: Samuel Bourne, Dilkusha Kothi, albumen print, December 1864–early 1865.

Chapter Three

THE 'COUNTRY HOUSES' OF LUCKNOW

Neeta Das

U ntil the fifteenth century, English nobles lived in fortified castle towns, which were designed both for living and security. But when peace prevailed in the country, the rule of force was replaced by the rule of law. Security became a less important factor in house design and castles became redundant, giving way to a new 'power house': the country house. It could work at the local level as a 'manor house', or at the national level as the seat of a Member of Parliament. People who lived in such houses were either powerful or rich, or both, with an interest in real estate, and thus country houses became visible evidence of power and wealth. The country houses were large, elaborate structures with rooms for lavish living, entertaining and pleasure. Until the seventeenth century the English country house continued to be built around two or more courtyards. Increasingly, however, with the influence of Italian and French architecture, there was a tendency to do without courtyards and cohere the building into a single symmetrical mass.[1] The idea of symmetry and order in architecture was carried further with the influence of Palladian 'villas',

Fig. 103: Captain J. Milliken, Dilkusha Kothi, east entrance, with stable and kitchen blocks on either side, albumen print, 3 April 1858.

Fig. 104: Felice Beato, Dilkusha Kothi, albumen print, 1858.

Dilkusha Kothi

Having bought the newly renamed Farhat Bakhsh, ready-built and located at one end of Hazratganj, Saadat Ali Khan's attention turned to the other end of the road. The site and location of Dilkusha Kothi suggest not only that it was intended to mark the end of this triumphal way but that it was also to serve as a hunting lodge and a country seat for the nawab. Saadat Ali Khan's aspiration for a country house, which he could use for entertaining and to which he could retire, in a culture where the concept of a country house was then unknown, might have been influenced by the French Governor's Ghirrety House outside Chandernagore, near Calcutta.[15]

It is evident that the nawab both loved his Persian traditions and was impressed by the Europeans. He therefore needed an architect who was well versed both in Persian and European culture to fulfil his dreams and ambitious plans. He found such a man in his aide-de-camp and friend, Major Gore Ouseley, who had previously served as the Company's Acting Resident in Lucknow. Ouseley had been born in Wales in 1770 and went to India in a military capacity. He was later appointed British Ambassador to the court of the shah of Persia in 1809. He was a scholar and connoisseur of oriental culture, ardently collecting oriental artefacts including books, paintings, musical instruments, rare gems and medals. He returned to England in July 1815 and was a founding member of the Royal Asiatic Society in London in 1823. He was also appointed a Fellow of the Antiquarian Society and assisted in establishing the Oriental Translation Society.

It was because of his knowledge of Persian culture that Gore Ouseley was entrusted with the task of fulfilling the nawab's architectural dream. Ouseley was, like most other architects of his time, an amateur. His education and training in architecture must have come from the study of the prolific European architectural publications of the seventeenth and eighteenth centuries, and from his extensive travels. What his education and experience would not include were construction techniques and building technology. For this he had to rely heavily on local craftsmen and masons, as did all amateur architects.

When Ouseley was faced with the problem of designing Dilkusha (which means 'heart-pleasing'), he chose a design that was 'befitting' to the status of the patron. The building was sited in a large wooded park and entrusted to the local craftsmen for execution (fig. 102). No known drawings of Dilkusha were made; however, considering the minuteness of detailing, it can be assumed that the palace was built under the strict supervision of the architect – it is highly improbable that the craftsmen of the region were familiar with the classical orders.[16]

The building that Gore Ouseley chose as a prototype for Dilkusha was Seaton Delaval, a country house in Northumberland, designed and built by Sir John Vanbrugh for Admiral George Delaval between 1717 and 1729. It was gutted by a fire in 1822, but its ruins still exist. The designs of Seaton Delaval were published in the third volume of Colin Campbell's *Vitruvius Britannicus* in 1725 (fig. 105). Of the 238 buildings represented in the three volumes of *Vitruvius Britannicus*, it is important to investigate why Seaton Delaval was chosen by architect and patron as the prototype for the new palace in Lucknow.

A number of formal principles are present in both Seaton Delaval and traditional Islamic structures: the centralized and symmetrical main structure, the placing of this structure at the head of major axes of the entrance courts, and the frontal approach. In both cases, the courts are enclosed by colonnades and can be reached along either the major or minor axes, and approached through entrance gates. In Islamic architecture, the most common examples of this layout are the tombs of the Mughal emperors and the imambaras of the nawabs. Thus the design of Seaton Delaval, with landscaped gardens on one front and large courts on the other, brought together the interests and predilections of both the English architect and the nawab. Whereas the architect chose the design based upon its appropriateness to the situation, the nawab was looking for familiar architectural forms. As in other aspects of their relationship, the design of Seaton Delaval offered the possibility of compromise between the two diverse cultures.

Once the nawab and Gore Ouseley had chosen Seaton Delaval as a model, and a site outside the city limits for the intended palace, the next step was to execute the building. Before doing this, however, Ouseley modified the design to suit the site and the wishes of his client (fig. 106). Ouseley placed the garden (or east) façade, with its great court, towards the Gomti, so the nawab could cruise down by boat and enter Dilkusha from the river side. The six-columned portico on the west façade was the 'town' entrance, for people coming from Lucknow. Other than this there are only minor differences between the drawings of Seaton Delaval and Dilkusha. The Palladian windows in the second floor of the side towers of Seaton Delaval were not repeated on the side faces of Dilkusha. Early photographs show that, unlike its English counterpart, a staircase led up from the north façade of the palace. Again, unlike Seaton Delaval, there is also an entry to the basement from the south façade, making the palace accessible from all four faces.

Vitruvius Britannicus included a plan and the two major façades of Seaton Delaval but did not reproduce any drawings of the kitchen and the stable blocks. Ouseley therefore had to provide supplementary designs for these, and in so doing ingeniously reflected the major elements of the building. For both blocks, he used a tripartite composition bounded by corner blocks similar to the stair towers of the main house. He continued the pattern of the ground floor and basement windows of the main house façade. The entrance to the court is representative of the façade facing the court, with the rusticated coupled Doric columns forming the gateway. By contrast, the rear façades of the blocks, facing away from the main building, are composed of the major elements of the tetrastyle Ionic portico, but this time with the pediments as in Seaton Delaval.

The rectangular plan of the stable block is divided into three longitudinal bays. The side bays are further subdivided to house the horses, whereas the central bay is left for circulation. Despite the basement and ground floor windows visible on its façade, the stable block is only one storey high. Entry to the stables from the road and the court is along its shorter axis. The stable block was connected to the main house by a high wall, but its location in plan is unclear. From the photographs one can deduce that its position might have been similar to that at Seaton Delaval, which is beyond the stair blocks. Nothing of the kitchen block, which stood opposite the stable block, remains today. It is only known from drawings and a single photograph (figs. 102 & 103).

Interestingly, the earliest illustration of Dilkusha (fig. 102), painted in 1814–15 by Sita Ram, shows that Ouseley's original conception was much nearer that of Seaton Delaval than it appears in mid-nineteenth-century photographs. Notably, the pointed, chapel-like roof at the top of the house, an important feature of Vanbrugh's plan, is shown in 1814 but had been removed by the 1850s. Conversely, the curious conical turrets on either side of the pediment are a later addition, as are the numerous statues at roof level.

Dilkusha, like any typical nawabi building, is made of solid-baked brick masonry walls, varying from two to five feet in thickness and covered with stucco. The walls are spanned by teak planks with thinner wooden planks laid on top. Across these joists are cemented two layers of pottery tiles, covered by four to five inches of rubble or mortar to create the floor, which is then plastered and polished. Floors such as this sometimes incorporated pottery ducts as a cooling device. It is uncertain whether Dilkusha employed this technique. Much stone is also employed in these buildings, especially at places where it will stop the damp rising from the ground, lintels and floors. The usual type of brick employed in Lucknow during the nawabi period is *lakhori*; these bricks are only three-quarters of an inch thick, and normally about four inches high and six inches long. The bricks are made of a fine local clay, with crystalline flecks, which turns a dull orange colour when baked. The great advantage of the thin *lakhori* bricks was that they could be used both in conjunction with larger bricks and by themselves to form fine details, even before the stucco was applied. This technique was used to make the circular columns and the heavy rustication of Dilkusha before these features were covered with stucco.[17] The stucco itself was made from a type of lime called *chunam*, mixed with lentils, shells and gum. The stucco work was done by means of specially shaped trowels rather than moulds or stamps.

Pottery, too, was extensively used in buildings for decorative purposes during the nawabi period. Potters soon learnt that balustrades, roof finials, clay medallions and ornaments could be imitated in clay, and later glazed or gilded. At Dilkusha, the statues and ornaments decorating the roofline were made of pottery, while the conical caps of the stair towers were made from wooden 'shells' covered with gilded metal. The latter was also a common technique employed during the nawabi period to make cupolas and domes.[18]

Dilkusha Kothi (fig. 88) was the backdrop to both the private and public life of the nawabi court. It served as the starting point of ceremonial processions – which might celebrate the birth, wedding or coronation ceremony of any member of the royal family, as well as religious festivals or the arrival of a distinguished guest. Dilkusha served occasionally as a guest house for European officers. At other times it was used as a hunting lodge by the nawab, usually accompanied by his Indian and English friends. Sometimes the nawab would stay there for a couple of days before going out on an expedition. The court would then move out to the nearby woods to hunt for animals, most of which were specially stocked for such hunts.[19] At these times the nawab would bring with him an extensive household, which included his *zenana* (women members of his family), friends and servants.

The palaces of the nawabs were expected to fulfil a wide range of functions. A palace such as this would include the ruler's private apartments, *zenana*, kitchens, quarters for bodyguards and servants, stables for the animals, baths and latrines for both sexes, and provide for other domestic needs.[20] Whereas the traditional palaces were spatially very complex, Dilkusha was a centrally organized structure with a simple, symmetrical plan. It took the ingenuity of Gore Ouseley to transform this simple plan so that it could accommodate the complex hierarchies that existed in the nawabi household. His basic solution was to manipulate the building into a four-sided structure with an entrance on

every side, thus offering at least four major and distinct movement patterns: for the nawab, his begums, his visitors and his servants. Also, instead of using a traditional horizontal palace layout Ouseley stacked the spaces vertically, in the order of their use and importance. In this way he could accommodate the complete functional requirements of a nawabi palace.

Spatial functions within Dilkusha can be identified with the help of William Knighton's descriptions of the various rooms during his stay at the palace. According to his account, on the ground or entrance floor there was a waiting area for visitors, a billiards room and a small room used as a guest bedroom. On the same floor there was the fifty-foot long dining room, big enough to accommodate the *nautch*, or dances.[21] Ladies of the royal and upper class families were carried in covered palanquins. The east entrance of Dilkusha (fig. 103), with its room projecting into the garden, would seem ideal for the palanquin-borne begums. It is probable that the sleeping quarters of the nawab and the *zenana* were on the first floor level, because the space on the ground floor seems insufficient for more than one person. The rooms on the south-east corner of the first floor were probably the bedchambers of the nawab and the begums, whereas the other rooms would be used as treasury, dressing and storage spaces.

The nawab would enter through the gateway of the stable block from the north side, where his elephants and horses could be kept after he had dismounted. He would then enter the main palace and either await his visitors (without having to mingle with them) in his *durbar* (audience hall), or continue to the retiring room beyond. The west end thus became a part of the royal domain.

The visitor would arrive at the prominent west entrance (fig. 104), and would wait in the long hall to be summoned by the nawab. On being summoned, he would enter the audience hall to see the nawab seated on his gilded chair at one end of the long room, and politely wait his turn. At the opposite end would be the dining table. The description of dining rooms by Knighton suggests that the nawab sat in the middle of the longer side of the table, while the guests sat on the two shorter ends. In this way they could enjoy entertainment provided by jugglers, pantomine-artistes, snake charmers, puppeteers, musicians and dancers, while they dined.[22]

Servants were an indispensable part of court life, and their movement was both flexible and necessary at all levels. An entrance below ground level on the south side suggests that the basement accommodated the kitchen and other services. It is also probable that there was a staircase in the south-west turret leading from the basement to the upper floors; this would have been the servants' major vertical circulation route. Thus they would have been able to serve meals in the ground floor dining room, wait upon begums at the first floor level and supply hot and cold water to the roof level, which probably accommodated the *hammams* and the latrines. Before the modern sewage system came to India, latrines would be a raised chamber with a small hole in the floor and two footrests. The night soil was collected in a bucket at a lower level, to be removed later by a sweeper. Because of the unhygienic nature of the system, Indian toilets were located either on the service streets or as separate blocks in the compounds. As Dilkusha had neither, it seems likely that they were on the roof terrace. (Flues to dispose of terrace water, built into the masonry, are concealed behind the façade of many nawabi buildings.) A description of Barowen (Musa Bagh) by Viscount Valentia, written about 1803, states that 'on the roof is erected a range of small rooms, which occasionally serves as a zenana, being surrounded by a high parapet wall'.[23]

Very little is known about the interior decoration of nawabi palaces, although we have some idea about the furnishings found in the separate male and female quarters. Whereas the male areas tended to be Europeanized, the female spaces had more traditional and austere settings. Knighton describes a nawab's room as being generally large and 'ornamented with rich chandeliers and gaudily framed pictures in great numbers. Generally speaking, there was too great a crowding of objects … the effect was to bewilder, rather than please.'[24]

It is probable that all the *kothis* commissioned by Saadat Ali Khan were designed in a similar way to Dilkusha. All of them were European in style, although a number of different architects were employed. The buildings were probably carefully chosen from pattern books and executed with little or no change. However, some, such as Barowen (fig. 101) and Bibiapur, retained their purpose as country houses, whereas others served as city mansions. While Alam Bagh (fig. 111), commissioned by Wajid Ali Shah in 1850, retained the authenticity of the European traditions, the same cannot be said for the majority of *kothis* built after Saadat Ali Khan's reign.

The North front of Seaton Delaval in the County of Northumberland the Seat of Francis Delaval Esq.   design'd by Sr. Iohn Vanbrugh Kt. 1721.

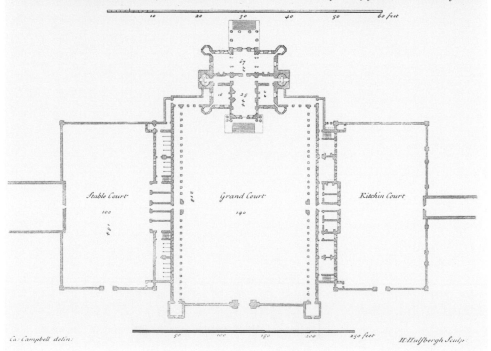

Stable Court

Grand Court

Kitchin Court

Ca: Campbell delin: H. Hulsbergh Sculp.

Fig. 105: Colin Campbell, Seaton Delaval, from *Vitruvius Britannicus, or the British Architect,*
engraving, 1717–25.

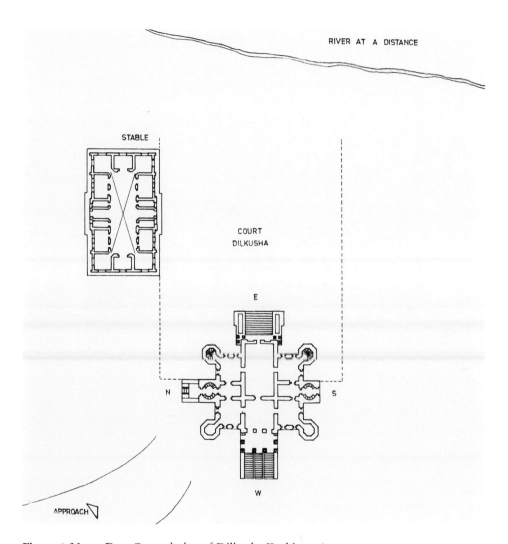

RIVER AT A DISTANCE

STABLE

COURT
DILKUSHA

E

N

S

W

APPROACH

Fig. 106: Neeta Das, Ground plan of Dilkusha Kothi, 1998.

Fig. 107: Darogha Ubbas Alli, Dilkusha Kothi, Plate 5 from *The Lucknow Album*, albumen print, 1860s, published 1874.

Fig. 108: John Edward Saché, Dilkusha Kothi, albumen print, c. 1867.

Fig. 109: Unknown photographer, Dilkusha Kothi, albumen print, 1880s.

Fig. 110: **Unknown photographer,** Dilkusha Kothi, garden façade, albumen print, 1870s.

Later *kothis*

None of the *kothis* that followed had the Palladian simplicity and geometric order of Dilkusha. The centralized layout did not suit the nawabs' lifestyle, and these buildings became increasingly 'Indianized', incorporating functions such as imambaras and mosques, which had a typical architectural style very different from that of the Europeans. Some even included courtyards. They also had multiple rooms laid out in a complex pattern: their façades continued to be 'European' in appearance, but the internal layout was totally changed. Unlike Dilkusha, where the architect tried to improvise while keeping the basic concept behind the building type intact, the new *kothis* had an intricate structure. A good example is Darshan Bilas, also called Chaurukhi Kothi, 'the house with four faces' (see Chapter One). This building had four façades, three of them imitating different buildings of Lucknow: Dilkusha, Barowen and Farhat Bakhsh respectively. Other examples are Roshan-ud-daula Kothi, Begum Kothi (which stood in Hazratganj, but is now demolished) and Taronwali Kothi (fig. 112). This last building was designed around 1830 during the reign of Nasir-ud-din specifically as an observatory for the British.[25] Today it is used by the State Bank of India.

The later *kothis* lost not only their basic planning and formal qualities but even the fundamental concept of a villa and country house. By and by, all large houses came to be known as *kothis*. Developed initially for the nawabs and the elite, this 'new' prototype dwelling could in due course be built for anyone who could afford a large house. But the influence of the original *kothis* was far-reaching. Twenty-first-century Lucknow is a result of the visionary town planning of Saadat Ali Khan and the 'transplanted' *kothis* such as Dilkusha. These houses, designed and executed by amateur architects like Martin and Ouseley, helped Lucknow become a modern city. The culture and layout of sixteenth- and seventeenth-century Lucknow had been essentially Indian: embedded within its dense and labyrinthine urban fabric were domestic houses of a similar form, with a central inner courtyard and multifunctional rooms – some covered, some semi-covered – all around. The villa-type *kothis* stood in marked contrast to these traditional residences. Thus, the first influence of the *kothis* was that free-standing houses came into vogue. The same building type, the villa-*kothi*, also came to be used for commercial and institutional buildings.

These free-standing, vertically stacked structures, with their dominant façades, were influential in another way: they demanded space around them from which they could be admired. This new building type greatly influenced urban morphology, demanding as it did a revision of traditional street patterns. The development of Hazratganj, with its grand *kothis*, brought about a new definition of urban space and city planning. The streets of 'new Lucknow' became wider, and the density of the subsequent new sectors became looser.[26]

Not only did the villa introduce a new building type, a new architectural vocabulary and a new understanding of urban space, but it brought with it the neo-classical ideals of the western world. The old rule of the Mughals was rejected and a search for the 'new' order began. In architecture, European ideals were substituted for the old order. Revivals and a pluralistic approach can be seen in the design of all the structures in this period. Buildings could feature more than just one style – indeed, the hybrid nature of the language became the 'style' of the period. The construction of buildings passed from the medieval masons into the hands of the new professionals, the architects. Medieval Lucknow slowly metamorphosed into neo-classical 'nawabi' Lucknow, and the modern city of today.

Fig. 111: **P. G. Fitzgerald,** Alam Bagh, albumen print, February 1858.

Fig. 112: **Felice Beato,** Taronwali Kothi (the Observatory), albumen print, 1858.

Fig. 113: G. W. Lawrie & Co., Ruins of the Residency, gelatin silver print, 1890s.

Chapter Four

THE RESIDENCY AND THE RIVER

Rosie Llewellyn-Jones

The city of Lucknow, former capital of Awadh, lies in the flat and fertile plains of northern India, on the River Gomti, itself a tributary of the great Ganges river. Today's casual travellers – here to pray at the Shia shrines, to visit the crumbling palaces of the nawabs or (more rarely these days) to pay their respects at the bullet-scarred Residency – will not at first be aware of the topographical features of the city. Only gradually do these become apparent when one ventures into the old city, and especially the Chowk, the principal street of the medieval city, which leads to the site of Macchi Bhawan. Here the hilly nature of the ground, although now thickly covered by buildings, becomes apparent. Joseph Tieffenthaler, the Jesuit priest and one of the first people to describe and draw Lucknow in 1765 (fig. 3), noted how visitors to the Chowk had to climb up and down steep stairs to access the buildings on either side. He described the Chowk as a gorge, while 'the greatest part of the town extends towards the east and covers an elevated place'.[1]

Apart from the Chowk – which seems to have followed the path of an old *nullah*, or dry stream bed, with its raised banks on both sides – there were three significant elevated areas in Lucknow. The advantages of building on even a slight incline in a riverine plain are evident: drainage, especially during the monsoon, is accelerated; cooling breezes are more effective; and attacks by enemies are more easily anticipated and repulsed. Macchi Bhawan, a fortress building and the principal home to the medieval rulers of Lucknow, the Sheikhzadas, stood proud upon a small hill directly south of the Gomti, rising above the river. The second adjacent site, where the Aurangzeb Mosque stands today, is Lakshman Tila, the hill that may have given the city its name. The third hill, a little way to the south-east, is the site of the British Residency.

The Residency and its Origins

The Residency complex (fig. 114) began to develop during the last quarter of the eighteenth century. Europeans felt that in India hilly areas were healthier than low-lying, marshy ground, which might hold dangerous miasmas. Initially only a few dwellings for Europeans were erected on the Residency site, and were built in a fairly piecemeal fashion. The eventual size of the Residency complex, covering 33 acres, could not have been imagined at its inception, any more than the six-month long siege of 1857, when its naturally hilly features were desperately fortified against the besiegers.

The appointment of the first British Resident to the court of Awadh was in 1773, when the nawab Shuja-ud-daula was persuaded by Warren Hastings, then the Governor of the Bengal Presidency (later Governor-General), to accept 'a person of trust' by him from the East India Company.[2] Nathaniel Middleton, a friend of Hastings, arrived in January 1774 to take up his appointment in Faizabad, then the nawabi capital. When Shuja-ud-daula's son, the nawab Asaf-ud-daula moved the capital back to Lucknow in 1775, the British Resident, now John Bristow, had to move too. At first there was no obvious site for the nascent Residency in Lucknow, and at

the time nothing more was needed than a decent house for one man and a couple of clerks. Although no correspondence exists, it is likely that John Bristow turned for advice to a friend who knew both Faizabad and Lucknow well.

Captain (later Major General) Claude Martin, had been in Faizabad as an officer of the East India Company, and possibly also in the service of Shuja-ud-daula.[3] Martin writes of having been associated with the nawabi court since the time of Shuja-ud-daula, and he was certainly more familiar with it than the newly appointed Bristow, who had formerly pursued an undistinguished career as a Company writer. Martin had had the advantage of being stationed in Lucknow earlier too, in 1765, when he was collecting land revenue. It is possible that he bought his first piece of land or property here during this period, a decade before prices rose. Certainly by the time he was appointed Superintendent of Asaf-ud-daula's arsenal in 1776, he was buying and renting houses in Lucknow.[4]

As a land surveyor for the East India Company, Martin would have appreciated the advantages of the hill as eminently suitable for European occupation. Tieffenthaler's map shows it as an elevated area with a couple of bungalows and palm trees (fig. 3). It was marked by the *mazaar* (shrine) of a Muslim saint and a few modest dwellings. It was near the river, well-wooded, and a mile or so distant from the city of Lucknow. It lay south-east of Macchi Bhawan Palace, close enough for communication between the Resident and the nawab's court, but not too close.

As the number of Residency staff increased, so did the buildings on the hill. By 1777, four years after the nawab had first agreed to accept a Resident at his court, John Bristow needed three bungalows for offices and his own accommodation and two bungalows for his assistants. Their cost, which the Company got the nawab to meet, was Rs 5,500.[5] A year later the Residency 'treasury', housed in a thatched bungalow, burnt down. Its contents, partly in gold coin, had been rescued from the burning building, but had to be 'guarded by Sepoys and lay in the open for many days'.[6] Nathaniel Middleton, now returned as Resident, then announced grandly that he had 'taken on me to direct the Erection of a strong brick building to serve as well the purpose of a Treasury as a safe Repository for the Records of my Office.'[7] A second, one-storeyed treasury was later erected which still stands today, just to the right of the main entrance through the Baillie Guard Gateway.

It was a time of rapid expansion, for in 1779 Middleton was asking for more money for 'necessary offices for the extensive business of the Department. ... these consisting chiefly of Bungalows and thatched places and having required continual repairs'.[8] By the time the artist Ozias Humphry arrived to spend the summer of 1786 in Lucknow, he was comfort-ably accommodated in the bungalow of John Wombwell, the Company's accountant. Wombwell had a pleasant bungalow at the north-west corner of the site, next to the Mound, a circular hill overlooking a small stream.[9] (The site of his bungalow can be identified today as the Inglis bungalow on maps of the Residency in 1857.) A drawing of the *zenana* near Mr Wombwell's bungalow, by Humphry, shows that the accountant had adopted the practice of keeping a *bibi*, or Indian mistress, with him. In fact Wombwell had so thoroughly assimilated himself into the life of a 'white Mughal', as such people have recently been styled, that he was painted in Indian dress, sitting on a *chaboutra* (low seat) on the bank of the Gomti, smoking a hookah.[10]

Fig. 114: Sita Ram, *Residency at Lucknow*, watercolour, 1814–15.

Fig. 115: **Unknown photographer,** Baillie Guard Gate, British Residency, albumen print, 1870s.

Fig. 116: **Unknown photographer,** The Banqueting Hall in the Residency compound, albumen print, 1870s.

Fig. 117:
Unknown photographer,
Imambara Sharaf-un-Nissan
and Masjid, adjacent to
the Begum Kothi, in the
Residency compound,
albumen print, 1870s.

Fig. 118:
John Edward Saché,
Monument to
'Sir Henry Lawrence
and Heroes',
albumen print, c. 1867.

Fig. 119: John Edward Saché, The spire of Christ Church seen from Wingfield Park, albumen print, c. 1867.

Fig. 120: Unknown photographer, Banqueting Hall seen from the Residency Tower, with the Chattar Manzil and Qaisarbagh beyond, albumen print, 1870s.

have been allocated to their many relatives, not all of whom are wealthy.

The river bank below the Residency hill is a cultivated area, prone to annual flooding. Behind it lies a long row of small houses and shops, called Kaptan Bazaar, which may be the bazaar referred to in Claude Martin's Will, built before he reached the rank of major general. A road leads from the shops to the Residency's Water Gate, useful for the British when they wanted to take a turn on the river. Less than a hundred yards east is Martin's town house, renamed by Saadat Ali Khan as Farhat Bakhsh, and now overshadowed by the adjoining Chattar Manzil, with its brass *chattars*, or parasols, shining in the sun. If the river is low, the basement floors of Farhat Bakhsh will be visible, their arched entrances shaded by *khus-khus tatties* (woven blinds of scented grass). Opposite stands Dilaram Kothi, with its pretty riverbank garden.

The pontoon bridge is swung open to let the boat sail through and the journey continues past Moti Mahal Palace, which covers almost as much ground as Chattar Manzil. Moti Mahal, or Pearl Palace, includes, apart from the main building, Shah Manzil and Mubarak Manzil. It was described as 'the beau ideal of a miniature citadel',[33] a fairy-tale castle with mock battlements, and the theme continued in its gateways with its toy soldier turrets and loopholes (fig. 18). Moti Mahal Palace was 'an extensive range of building abutting upon the river, and distinguished by a pavilion with four richly gilded domes. ... it is the prettiest building of the kind at Lucknow, spacious and airy'.[34] Built by the nawab Ghazi-ud-din Haider, the pavilion was designed to give the nawab's guests a grandstand view of the animal fights that were staged across the river in front of Hazari Bagh, a walled enclosure (see Map 2). The unhappy elephants, rhinoceros, bears and tigers that took part in these popular entertainments could be clearly seen from the palace balcony.

Further downriver is Shah Najaf, its shallow dome seen above the walled enclosure, with its handsome riverside entrance gate. Just beyond is the raised mound of Qadam Rasool, with the little pavilion on top. This is the last building that is visible from the river for some considerable distance. The boat now passes between fields and small villages on either bank until the slender column in front of La Martinière appears in the distance (fig. 125). The building itself now comes into view, with its fantastic skyline of statues and *chattris* and the quadrant arches at it summit. In the basement lies the body of its founder, Claude Martin, as yet undisturbed. Milling about on the school steps and river bank are the pupils, all boys, and no doubt planning another raid on their neighbour's pumpkin fields, an enduringly popular sport. The journey ends at Dilkusha Kothi, another European style 'country house' subtly transmuted to suit the nawabi taste in this city of illusion.

Fig. 121: Felice Beato, Steamboat shaped as a fish, and the nawab's pinnace *The Sultan of Oude* at the Bara Chattar Manzil, albumen print, 1858.

Fig. 122: Ahmad Ali Khan, Pavilions in the River Gomti, bridging the Summer Palace/Chattar Manzil and Dilaram Kothi, albumen print, c. 1856.

Fig. 123: Mushkoor-ud-Dowlah or Asghar Jan, Pavilion in the River Gomti, between the Summer Palace and Dilaram Kothi, albumen print, 1860s.

Fig. 124: Felice Beato, Bridge of boats over the River Gomti, the Chattar Manzil beyond, albumen print, 1858.

Fig. 125 Felice Beato, Bridge of boats over the River Gomti, La Martinière in the distance, albumen print, 1858.

Fig. 126: Alexis de La Grange, Two-part panorama showing (left to right) the Stone Bridge, Aurangzeb Mosque, the Rumi Darwaza and the Bara Imambara complex, albumen prints, 1849–51.

Fig. 127: Felice Beato, The Iron Bridge, with Hindu temple on the left, albumen print, 1858.

Fig. 128: Edmund David Lyon, La Martinière, albumen print, c. 1862.

Chapter Five

LA MARTINIÈRE:
AN ENLIGHTENED VISION

Nina David

One cannot do better than to begin with the description of W. H. Russell, war correspondent for *The Times,* on first catching sight of La Martinière. He described it as

'… the most curious structure I ever saw. At first glance one exclaims, 'How beautiful! What a splendid building!' at the second, 'Why, it must have been built by a madman!' At the distance of more than half a mile we can make out the eccentric array of statues, the huge lions' heads, the incongruous columns, arches, pillars, windows and flights of stairs leading to nothing, which are the distinguishing features of the Martinière.'[1]

Reactions to La Martinière continue to be the same today.

Let us look briefly at the story of its builder, Major General Claude Martin (1735–1800). Historiography has long since discounted the 'great man' theory and the role of accident in history, but Thomas Carlyle and the late British historian A. J. P. Taylor in particular never abandoned their

conviction that an individual could significantly change the course of events. Past schools of history – especially in the field of Indian studies – may have been superseded, but although 'subaltern studies' have occupied centre stage in recent years, many historians still exult when they see modern theorists reverting to the 'role of the individual' in history. From the eighteenth to the twenty-first century, the name of Claude Martin, founder of La Martinière, has endured. Martin was a typical representative of the Enlightenment, the European movement that revered individualist attitudes and questioned established religious thinking. Today, vindicated by history, we can trace the career of this extraordinary Frenchman, who made a name for himself in an array of different professions in Awadh, becoming something of a polymath and a European at home in an oriental setting. He is one of the most intriguing figures of nawabi Lucknow.

Martin is commemorated in the building Constantia (fig. 128), the central portion of La Martinière College, where he is buried well below ground level. Planned by him and begun by June 1796, Constantia is the largest European funerary monument in India. Martin always wished Constantia to be first of all his final resting place and secondly, a college. In his Will he instructed his executors

'... to keep Lackperra house or Constantia house as a college for instructing young men in the English language and taking care of my tomb which house was properly my reason for having built it wanting at first to make it for my tomb or monument and a house for school or college for learning young men the English language and Christian religion if they find themselves inclined, but as now the house is of such an extensive plan ...'[2]

Claude Martin arrived in Pondicherry in 1752 'a common soldier', as he described himself in his lengthy Will, though ironically he is remembered in India today primarily as an educationalist. He left specific instructions, in his quaint English, that every year 'a toast to be drinked in memorandom [sic] of the Foundator' by the college boys, and this is still done every year by the prizewinners at La Martinière. In fact all 2,500 of the boys currently at the college (which opened in 1845) commemorate every year as Founder's Day the anniversary of Martin's death on 13 September.

As part of his Enlightenment beliefs, Martin deliberately placed no restrictions of religion, caste or creed on the young men admitted to the college. He believed that a college for only one community would be divisive and contrary to the mixed environment that existed in Lucknow, his home for over twenty-five years. He allocated rooms for a chaplain or a *mulla* (a learned Islamic clergyman), to be 'attendant on the school's men' to teach them both English and Persian. Martin's intentions for the education of Indian boys were fully carried out by the successive principals of the college. Thirty-one years after its foundation, the principal reported that '... hundreds of thousands of rupees are spent on the education of Natives. ... an insignificant dole for Europeans and Eurasians'.[3]

The mystifying paradox of Claude Martin's persona – his contempt for 'blacks', as he called them, is recorded in a letter to his friend the artist Ozias Humphry in 1789 – is not borne out by his deeds.[4] In fact, it has been said that 'General Martin was nearly as Indianised as the Nawab was Europeanised, providing the European counterpart to the Nawab's cosmopolitanism'.[5]

Claude Martin and the Nawabs of Awadh

Early on in his career Claude Martin discovered that with the dwindling fortunes of the French in India, he would be more professionally secure in the English East India Company. What kind of a man was he? Primarily a soldier, he rose from the ranks, eventually to command the forces of the nawabs of Awadh. He was also placed in charge of the arsenal by Nawab Asaf-ud-daula. At the same time he was a businessman, property-owner, indigo-manufacturer, moneylender, connoisseur, lapidary, geographer, self-taught architect and eventually, a philanthropist.

Nothing better illustrates Claude Martin's social standing in Lucknow than the painting entitled *Colonel Polier and his Friends at Lucknow* by Johann Zoffany, the German artist who visited Lucknow in the 1780s (fig. 129). A copy of the painting hangs in the Blue Room of Constantia today; the original is in the Victoria Memorial Hall, Calcutta. It depicts the interior of an apartment, probably in Colonel Polier's house at Lucknow, with a group of nine figures. In the centre beyond a table, the artist is seated at an easel, painting a picture of an Indian landscape, while five other pictures hang on the wall behind. Claude Martin is to the right of the picture, in scarlet military coat and holding dividers in his right hand. By his side (in blue coat and riding boots) is John Wombwell, an accountant of the East India Company. An Indian servant holds a depiction (identified as a painting by William Hodges) of Martin's town house, Lakh-e-pera (compare with fig. 17). Antoine-Louis Polier is to the left of the picture, in scarlet uniform and fur hat, giving orders to his Indian cook, who is showing a basket of fruits and vegetables. Two Indians play with the artist's favourite monkey in the background.

Martin also appears, with Asaf-ud-daula and other nobles and Europeans, in a second painting by Zoffany, entitled *Colonel Mordaunt's Cock Match* (fig. 2). Martin had a poor opinion of his employer, however, describing Asaf-ud-daula in derisory terms. He expressed no sorrow when the nawab died in 1797, but saw his death merely as an opportunity for the Company to lay hands on his vast fortune.[6] But whatever Martin's private opinion of the nawab, the fact remains that when he was appointed to his service, 'his days of wealth, prosperity and power' began.[7]

Martin's status was confirmed during the short tenure of the next nawab, Wazir Ali (r. September 1797 to January 1798), when he was requested by Sir John Shore, the Governor General of India, to prepare a spare tent for the nawab, which had a 'separate audience apartment and a partitioned wall around it'. In fact the 'Tarikh-e-Saadat', an unpublished Persian manuscript, states that Claude Martin was present at the enthronement of Wazir Ali and enjoyed parallel status with the British Resident G. F. Cherry. And at the enthronement of Nawab Saadat Ali Khan, just four months

Fig. 129: Johann Zoffany, *Colonel Polier and his Friends at Lucknow*, oil painting, 1786/87.

later, in January 1798, the author of the manuscript, Munshi Imam Baksh 'Bedaar', refers to the martial qualities of Claude Martin and to 'his bounteous nature, above that of all other Europeans present in the Awadh court of the times'.[8]

Claude Martin as Builder and Architect

The number of buildings designed or erected by Claude Martin in Lucknow is not known but he is likely to have had some involvement in the design of Asaf-ud-daula's new palace, Daulat Khana (fig. 16), which was finished about 1789. The arsenal that Martin built and superintended for the nawab was located where the present Raj Bhawan now stands (fig. 130). For a time this building was known as 'Banks' Bungalow' after the Chief Commissioner of Lucknow, Major John Sherbrooke Banks, who lived here in 1856. It was in this foundry, which may form the lower ground floor of the present building, that Martin cast the bronze cannon and large bell, dated 1786 and bearing his name, that is now placed outside the main entrance to La Martinière. The bell was restored to the college by the Allahabad Arsenal in 1871 and so does not appear in any of the photographs illustrating this chapter, many of which are of an earlier date.[9]

It was as an 'engineer-architect' that Claude Martin made his mark in eighteenth-century Awadh. He had had no formal training in either profession, although architecture was the subject of many of the volumes in his rich library at Lucknow. Some of the books are reflective of his interest in Etruscan, Egyptian and British architecture, which undoubtedly influenced his building style. His library included *The Builders Magazine, or Monthly Companion for Architects, Carpenters, Masons, Bricklayers etc. Consisting of designs in Architecture in every style and taste* (1774), *Travels through Syria and Egypt in 1783* by the Comte de Volney, and *Bucks Antiquities, or, Venerable remains of above four hundred Castles, Monasteries, Palaces, etc. in England and Wales, with near one hundred views of Cities and chief Towns* (1774) by Samuel and Nathanial Buck.[10] The title page of *The Builders Magazine* refers to 'Plans, Elevations and Sec-

tions, in the Greek, Roman and Gothic Taste'. This probably was the main source for the mixture of architectural styles employed by him in La Martinière. Philip Miller's book on plants, *Figures of the most beautiful, useful and uncommon plants described in the Gardeners Dictionary to which are added their descriptions, and an account of the classes to which they belong* (1760), also found a place on his shelf. It illustrates beautiful and uncommon plants and may have influenced Claude Martin's layout of his vast gardens with its rare plants and tree-*topes* (orchards).

Around 1795 Martin, long in the employ of the East India Company, decided to accept Lucknow as his final home rather than return to Europe as some of his contemporaries had done. Deeply affected by the violent death in 1795 of his friend Antoine-Louis Polier in France, and the departure to England in 1797 of another old friend, General Benoît de Boigne,[11] Martin settled for good in the place he had known since 1765. Now well established as an intermediary between the nawabi court and the British Residents, he began his plans for a 'country retreat'. His military services for Asaf-ud-daula during the second Rohilla War (1794), and the honours subsequently heaped on him, including the title of Major General, by the East India Company, meant that he would not now be transferred away from Lucknow.

Fig. 130: **Unknown photographer,** 'Banks' Bungalow', formerly Claude Martin's arsenal, also known as Hayat Bakhsh Kothi, albumen print, c. 1856.

There are many similarities in construction between Lakh-e-pera – Martin's town house – and Constantia. Both had deep basements, both were built on or near the River Gomti, and both were defensive buildings, with interesting roof-lines. Both buildings used water in inventive ways, at Lakh-e-pera to cool the basement storeys and at Constantia to supply cool air to the building, via a framework of four wells sunk at water level.

Constantia, as La Martinière was referred to by Claude Martin, does not belong to any school of architecture. It has perplexed experts, historians, visitors and laypersons over the centuries. Its size never ceased to awe critics, yet it produced a feeling of revulsion in George Annesley, Viscount Valentia, when he visited it in 1803.[12] He declared:

'It is a strange, fantastical building of every species of architecture and adorned with minute stucco fret-work, enormous red lions with lamps instead of eyes, Chinese mandarins and mythology. ... It has a handsome effect at a distance, from a lofty tower in the centre with four turrets; but on a nearer approach, the wretched taste of the ornaments only excites contempt. A more extraordinary combination of Gothic towers, and Grecian pilasters, I believe, was never before devised. He bequeathed it to the public as a *serai* [lodging house], every stranger being permitted to take up his residence there for two months.'

Bishop Reginald Heber, visiting Lucknow in 1824, was another critic. He continued, like others before him, to voice his distaste over the style of architecture adopted by Claude Martin. He noted:

'Another popular drive is to Constantia, a very large and most whimsical house and grounds in the worst possible taste, but displaying in its outlines and some part of its arrangements, an eccentric and uneducated genius, built by the late General Martin ...'[13]

A later visitor, the German captain, Leopold von Orlich, described it thus in 1845:

'In a desolate mangoe-garden, four miles to the south of the city, near to the river is a large, shapeless palace, called Constantia, which was erected by Claude Martin, the Frenchman. ... Constantia, which is five stories high, is built of marble, sandstone and bricks; it is a medley of the French, Italian and Greek styles, combined with Hindoo and Mahometan architecture, and has two towers, which stand on either side of the platform; the battlements and towers are adorned with colossal lions.'[14]

Claude Martin had always apprehended an 'Asiatick' attack, after his first town house was threatened during a brief rebellion by the Raja of Benares, Chait Singh, in 1781, and so Constantia was begun as a defensive structure. S. C. Hill, one of Claude Martin's earliest biographers, has referred to Martin's fondness for defensive buildings and quotes Thomas Twining's description of Constantia as a 'mansion' constructed with a view to defence, 'with drawbridges ... and turrets' (fig. 135).[15] But despite such adverse reactions, what has endured over the centuries is the feeling of reverence on the part of students for their Alma Mater. Generations of them have carved their initials on the steps of this magnificent building.

The parapets and pavilions of Martin's singular building reveal a hybrid design of statues of Greco-Roman goddesses (fig. 139). Twelve heraldic lions, in threatening stance, have niches in them, possibly used for *mashaals* (flaming torches) to ward off invaders. French shepherdesses abound, alongside figurines with musical instruments and an Egyptian sphinx for company (fig. 138). A late nineteenth-century guidebook, in a similar vein to earlier accounts, described it as 'a bizarre superstructure, chiefly remarkable for the superimposition of one of the Grecian Orders upon another ... crenellations varied by lions ... high over all rises the central tower crowned with a belvedere and flagstaff supported by flying buttresses'.[16] Statuary can be seen in all the photographs of La Martinière taken between late 1857 and 1874.

Visionary architect that he was, Claude Martin anticipated that no one would be able to replicate his efforts at building.

He shared his thoughts with Mrs Elizabeth Plowden, the wife of his old friend Captain Plowden, in a letter dated 5 June 1796.[17] Of particular interest is the description of Constantia on the bank of the River Gomti (fig. 125). He wrote:

'I have begun a house at my *tope* (Constantia Grove) … I am constantly there every morning on horse back and every afternoon in carriages after dinner, that building I think improve my health by making me take plenty exercise, as it is or will be a large pile of masonry, it will keep me long at it and perhaps as long as I live, if any accident happened to me, or otherwise I will have the happiness to see it finished and to hear people praise it, as they do my present one. Our Nabob is building everyday houses, palaces, gardens and copy everyone's house but I don't think he will ever be able to copy mine, he often demanded plan of my present house on the water. … As for my new one at Constantia Grove, I don't think he will ever attempt it. He has not seen it yet …'

The *Oudh Gazetteer* goes on to say that General Claude Martin 'designed the plan and elevation of it and showed them to Asaf-ud-daula who expressed a desire to buy it, and offered to give a million sterling for it', but the nawab's death in 1797 pre-empted that.[18]

As an added safeguard, Martin decreed that he should be buried in the basement at Constantia. (Usually, burial of a body in a building prevents confiscation of the building.) He gave clear instructions in his Will to his faithful servants, 'Mutchoo' and 'Chota' Qadir, that they should serve as *darogas* (superintendents) of the Constantia building and assume responsibility for the upkeep of his tomb within it. The direct descendant of 'Chota' Qadir, Mr Nur-ul-Azeem, has been the hereditary senior *daroga* since 1947, while his son Zia is the caretaker of La Martinière. Moin Ali, a collateral descendant of 'Mutchoo', carries on the unbroken tradition of seeing to the upkeep of the building.[19]

Claude Martin died in his town house, Lakh-e-pera, on 13 September 1800. His body was embalmed and buried in the vault prepared for it at Constantia, as he had directed in his Will. In Article Twenty-seven he wrote: 'My house at Luckperra or Constantia House is never to be sold as it is to serve as a monument or a tomb for to deposit my Body in.'[20]

At his death Martin was the wealthiest European in Awadh. He had lived so long in India that he chose not to be buried in the European funerary tradition – with the tomb raised above ground level, as in a cathedral or church – but in the Muslim fashion, below ground.

The Building of Constantia

Constantia's eclectic style defies description in classical architectural terms. The central tower is topped by intersecting arches. In the arrangement of its terraces and its 'castellar mass', as the Marquess of Hastings put it, 'an allusion to some eighteenth-century palaces of the English classical Baroque style' can be made, but there was no single precedent in British architectural history that might have served as its model.[21] Constantia contained Indian elements such as *chattris* (pavilions), which can be seen in all the photographs, and 'unique elements like the canopy of the balcony which resembles a spread cusped arch'.[22] Statues on the 'lantern' (apex) of Constantia were laid out in profusion, but many of them were destroyed during the earthquakes of 1803 and 1934.

The original materials employed in the construction of Constantia were brick, lime mortar and lime stucco; stucco was also elaborately used in the ceilings. Martin's inventory mentions slabs of Chunar stone for use in the house, and extensive marble slabs. Special bricks made by him and stamped 'F' are called *pan patta* and are slightly bigger than standard bricks. Curved and triangular bricks were utilized for balustrades and columns, the material of which is 'local fine clay with crystalline quart flecks and silt, fired at 600 degrees – 700 degrees C to get a dull orange colour'.[23] The mortar was a mixture of *kankar* lime, made from *urad ki daal* (ground lentils) and *gur* (crystallized sugar cane juice), to which was added *surkhi* (a reddish powder obtained from red brick stone).

Fig. 131: Sita Ram, *View of Constantia from the West* [La Martinière], watercolour, 1814–15.

Limestone from Katni was used for battlements, floors and stairs, and as reinforcement for statues. While meticulously planning out Constantia, a recently discovered letter written by Claude Martin himself from Lucknow throws light on his desire for the use of coloured marble squares 'to make up two octagons about twelve feet in diameter and one room about 45 feet long by 25 feet wide – oblong'.[24] Marble was a favourite material of Martin's, but many of the floors at Constantia were destroyed during the Revolt of 1857. Pottery was extensively used for decorative purposes, as shown in the small clay medallions of imitation Wedgwood in the present Library and Chapel. These raised ground-floor rooms were originally reception rooms, designed by Martin with symmetrical axes to maximize the slightest breeze.

It is unclear why Claude Martin called the building 'Constantia', but he had already adopted the motto *Labore et Constantia* ('Toil and Fidelity') by the 1780s. He had this inscribed in marble on the first floor of the building, facing the river and the artificial tank (fig. 140).

As discussed above, Martin left detailed instructions regarding his own burial at Constantia. It is interesting to note that he also provided for the *zenana* of his seven Indian mistresses, two of them sisters, all of whom outlived him.[25] He also left instructions for the building of tombs for two of his mistresses. His favourite 'girl' was Boulone Lize, and her simple, square *maqbara* (tomb) is near Constantia (fig. 132). Also known as Gori Bibi ('the fair lady'), she was a Muslim girl who had been adopted by Martin when she was about nine years old (fig. 133). Ample financial provision was made for her and her companions by Claude Martin. He stated in his Will that his property should be particularly given to the girl 'named Boulone or Lise for whom I have the greatest regard and affection'. She had been worthy of 'gratitude and services' rendered to him, and Claude Martin wrote of his 'regard' and 'satisfaction' with her. Out of deference for the customs of Lucknow society, and mindful of the prevalent *purdah* system, he also desired that when Boulone and Sally (another mistress) would visit his tomb then 'every man must be drawn away from the house'.[26]

In contrast, Martin's friend Antoine-Louis Polier in his Will left the care of his three *bibis* to Martin, and for a period of almost five years they lived in his *zenana*, with his own mistresses. Martin also left them small pensions in his Will, showing himself to be more generous than Polier, who appeared not to have made financial provision for them on his return to France. A son by one of Polier's mistresses, a boy called George, was later sent by Martin to live in England with the former wife of another friend, Benoît de Boigne.[27] These men shrank from disclosing their Indian shenanigans in European society: no better example exists than Polier, who abandoned his native 'black' offspring without remorse. Only dutiful letters are left behind to his mistresses as proofs of his Indian dalliance. In Claude Martin's case, he was infertile, so the question of heirs did not arise. He made bequests to his mistresses, but the bulk of his fortune went to the founding of La Martinière schools.

As for Martin's own burial, his Will instructed that he was to be interred at Constantia 'in the small round room north easterly' (that is, on a north–east axis), with the tomb 'two

Fig. 132: **Unknown photographer,** The Tomb of Boulone Lize, with La Martinière in the background, albumen stereoscopic print (detail), March/April 1858.

Fig. 133: Johann Zoffany, *Boulone Lize, Claude Martin's Favourite Mistress,* oil painting, c. 1786.

In the 1870s, high floods of the Gomti had inundated the ground floor and the wings of La Martinière, so much so that the arches under the *lath* were completely submerged (fig. 142). By 1878 the Principal, T. G. Sykes, reported that the entire structure was very much in need of repairs and five years later, on 31 March 1883, he expressed his concern for Martin's tomb.[41] In 1881 the straight wings were made double-storeyed, and the dairy and stables were constructed on the estate in 1893. By 1895 a covered passage linked the two wings to the central building.

As a structure, La Martinière underwent the usual repairs. Floods, like those of 1971, played havoc with the building, causing drastic changes in the topography on the *lath* side as can be seen when we compare the present state with what is revealed in nineteenth-century photographs of the building and its surroundings. A *bund* (embankment) was erected between the building and the lake in the 1970s, but the visual connection of Constantia and the *lath* was lost as a result. Today the lake has silted up due to the drainage of the catchment area having been cut off, and it is now impossible to view La Martinière as a 'distinct' horizontal expanse from the base of the *lath* as one does in earlier photographs.

In 1872 an attempt was made to revive 'Constantia Grove', when the Principal, Mr Stobart, referred to the 'afforestation' of the area.[42] Photographs from this period also indicate that the corridors, which now link the principal building to the wings on either side, had not yet been constructed (fig. 136).

The Need for Conservation

La Martinière is both a historic edifice and an architectural wonder, and conservation experts rightly feel an urgent need for the preservation of the building and its surrounding 700 acres of land. Today, it needs about £100,000 just to begin restoration. A report by INTACH (the Indian National Trust for Art and Cultural Heritage) has identified four 'layers' in La Martinière, which highlight the different kinds of materials, techniques and architectural styles used in its construction. The first layer comprises the basement, ground floor and first floor, all of which were built during Claude Martin's lifetime. Expensive materials were used during this period but were removed during the Revolt. Interestingly, traces of iron bars have been identified in the basement, one of the earliest examples of reinforcement in a brick building. The second layer includes the central tower built under the supervision of Mutchoo and Chota Qadir. The third layer comprises changes that date to between 1844 and 1947, a period that saw many additions, such as the arcades of 1896 and the stained glass windows, wooden screens and marble tiles introduced into the Chapel in the 1890s. Layer four, post-1947, was dominated by repair and maintenance work, where the use of cement and modern bricks was predominant. The continued use of cement in repairs today is damaging the building: lime mortar is to be preferred, as it facilitates the evaporation of moisture.[43]

Despite all its problems, both physical and aesthetic, Constantia survives today as a much-loved building. Claude Martin's brilliant masterstrokes – the decision that he be buried in La Martinière, and his founding of an educational institution based on secular values – have undoubtedly paid off.

Fig. 134: Frith's Series, La Martinière and the *lath*, albumen print, 1870s.

Fig. 135:
Frith's Series,
La Martinière,
albumen print,
mid-1870s.

Fig. 136: Frith's Series, La Martinière and the *lath*, albumen print, 1870s.

Fig. 137: **Unknown photographer,** La Martinière, albumen print, c. 1880.

Fig. 138:
Sphinx on the
first-floor roof,
La Martinière,
winter 1975–76.

Fig. 139:
Classical statues
on the first-floor roof,
La Martinière,
winter 1975–76.

Fig. 140:
The river façade with Martin's motto *Labore et Constantia* ('Toil and Fidelity') above the first-floor balcony, La Martinière, winter 1975–76.

Fig. 141: **Samuel Bourne,** La Martinière, garden side, albumen print, December 1864–early 1865.

Fig. 142: Unknown photographer, La Martinière and the *lath*, albumen print, 1870s.

Fig. 143: **Unknown photographer,** La Martinière and the *lath*, view across the Tank, albumen print, 1870s.

BIOGRAPHIES OF THE PHOTOGRAPHERS

Stéphanie Roy

Abbas Ali, Darogah (Darogha Ubbas Alli) *Indian*
(active 1860s–70s)
Amateur photographer

A municipal engineer in Lucknow, Ubbas Alli (as he styled himself) was probably trained at the Thomason Engineering College, Roorkee, which from 1864 offered photographic instruction to Indians in order to help them record the progress of public works projects. In 1874 Ubbas Alli produced a photographically illustrated book entitled *The Lucknow Album* (G. H. Rouse, Baptist Mission Press, Calcutta). It contained fifty albumen prints, many of which were made in the 1860s, which documented the architecture of Lucknow. In the book's introduction, Ubbas Alli observed that 'the volume may be preserved, for transmission to posterity, as a memorial of the dangers passed and the hardships suffered by the glorious Garrison of Lucknow', thus emphasizing the historical importance of the publication. The same year, twenty-four photographs depicting dancing girls of Lucknow were published in a volume entitled *The Beauties of Lucknow*, attributed to Ubbas Alli by the historian P. C. Mookherjee. In 1880 he published *An Illustrated Historical Album of the Rajas and Taaluqdars of Oudh* (Allahabad), a book containing 250 *carte-de-visite* portraits of the Awadh aristocracy.

Ahmad Ali Khan, 'Chhote Miyan' *Indian*
(active 1850s–1860s)
Amateur photographer

In 1883, the writer P. C. Mookherjee described Ahmad Ali Khan as the designer of Husainabad Imambara and the Qaisarbagh complex. Known as the *daroga* (superintendent) of Husainabad Imambara, he took up photography c. 1853. By 1856 he had produced an extensive series of portraits of both European and Indian residents of Lucknow, including the last nawab, Wajid Ali Shah, the royal children and the ladies of the court, as well as the photographer J. C. A. Dannenberg (q. v.). Khan's architectural views of Lucknow are less well known, but are extremely important as historical documents. Ahmad Ali Khan's view of the Qaisarbagh was used by Martin Gubbins as the basis of a lithograph that served as the frontispiece to his book *An Account of the Mutinies in Oudh, and of the Siege of the Lucknow Residency* (London 1858). Other photographs were the basis of engravings reproduced in *The Illustrated Times* and the *Illustrated London News* in 1858. After the 1857 uprising he continued to practise photography, employing the alias 'Chhote Miyan'. He became a member of the Bengal Photographic Society in 1862, and some of his views were exhibited at the Society's annual exhibition the same year. His photographs were also displayed in the 1885 exhibition in Lucknow. The accompanying catalogue described him as 'the first person in India who, after learning this art in 1270 AH [AD 1853–54], practised and spread it in Oudh' (Mustafai Matba', *Qatrah-I Muheet-I Bahr-I Hind*, Lucknow 1885, p. 15).

Asghar Jan *Indian* (active 1860s)
Commercial photographer

During the 1860s, Asghar Jan, brother of Mushkoor-ud-Dowlah (q. v.) was a recognized commercial photographer in Lucknow. Mentioned in P. C. Mookherjee's *Pictorial*

Lucknow of 1883, Asghar Jan worked alongside his brother; their names appear together in their studio's ink-stamp found on the reverse of the photographs.

Beato, Felice *Greek/British* (1834–c. 1907)
Commercial photographer

Felice Beato started his photographic career in the Middle East, working in partnership with James Robertson between 1853 and 1857. He is believed to have travelled to Russia twice, once in 1855 to cover the final stages of the Crimean conflict, and again in 1856 to photograph its aftermath following the conclusion of peace. His experiences in the Crimea marked the beginning of his career as a war photographer. On hearing of the Uprising of 1857 Felice sailed to Calcutta, reaching the city on 13 February 1858. During 1858 his brother Antonio joined him, arriving from Egypt and basing himself in a studio in Calcutta. Felice applied to the East India Company for permission to visit the stricken cities of Lucknow, Cawnpore and Delhi. A permit was issued on 16 March 1858, reading 'A licence to Felix Beato, 24 years old, with two Maltese servants, a native of Corfu, to proceed to Lucknow and other places for eight months'. Beato also photographed in Benares, Amritsar and Lahore – cities unaffected by the Revolt of 1857. In December 1859 Antonio left India for Egypt to establish his own photographic business there. Felice sailed for Hong Kong in February 1860 with Sir Hope Grant, Commander of the British forces in China, to document the Anglo-Chinese War. A catalogue of his Indian and Chinese photographs was published by the London art dealer Henry Hering, listing over three hundred images. Through this work Beato gained some considerable renown as a war photographer, with images that were emotionally powerful, such as the famous view of the interior of the Sikander Bagh showing skeletons of Indian soldiers in the foreground. In November 1861, Beato returned to London, and his movements are unclear until June 1863, when he is known to have arrived in Japan, where he remained until 1885. He initially established a partnership called Beato & Wirgman, Artists &

Photographers in Yokohama with his friend the British artist Charles Wirgman, whom he had met in China, but Beato later went on to operate his own business, F. Beato & Company, between 1869 and 1877. In November 1866, a major fire in Yokohama claimed much of his stock of images, and Beato appears to have spent the following year trying to replace the lost photographs. In 1877, he sold his entire studio, including his stock of negatives, to Baron Raimund von Still-fried's Japan Photographic Association. He was appointed Honorary Consul for Greece in Japan in 1873. James Robertson and his family joined Beato in 1882 in Yokohama. Beato also worked in Korea in 1871, accompanying the United States naval expedition to Kanghwado. He was briefly in the Sudan in 1885, to photograph the Mahdist rebellion against the British, and moved to Burma two years later, where it is believed he remained until his death c. 1907.

Bourne, Samuel *British* (1834–1912)
Commercial photographer

While working as a bank clerk in the 1850s, Bourne took up photography as an amateur, photographing buildings and landscapes in and around Nottingham. He made excursions to the Lake District, Wales and probably Scotland, producing accomplished topographical and architectural views. In 1862 he gave up his work at the bank and travelled to India, arriving in January 1863. Initially disappointed by Calcutta, he quickly reached Simla, where he set up his studio in partnership with a Mr Howard, as 'Howard & Bourne'. Later the same year Charles Shepherd, of the firm Shepherd & Robertson (q. v.), arrived in Simla and joined the partnership, creating Howard, Bourne & Shepherd. By 1865 the business had become Bourne & Shepherd. Two additional studios were subsequently established, in Calcutta (1867) and Bombay (1870). Bourne is particularly known for the three expeditions he undertook in the Himalayas. His first and second trips, conducted in 1863 and 1864, covered the Himalayan foothills near Simla and Kashmir; the third trip, in 1866, is now famous for the trek through Spiti and Bourne's views of the Manirung Pass at an altitude of 18,600 feet. Each of his expeditions was carefully described in a series of letters published in *The British Journal of Photography*. Bourne produced a series of Lucknow views shortly after he returned from his second trek, between December 1864 and early 1865. He returned briefly to England in 1867 to marry Mary Tolley. He visited South India where he recorded the Hindu temples of Tamil Nadu and the hill station of Ootacamund. In 1870 Bourne left India to settle in Nottingham, where he built up a highly successful cotton doubling business. He continued to photograph as an amateur, producing views of his travels in the south of France. Bourne was also a talented amateur watercolourist, and he exhibited his work in local art exhibitions.

Clifton & Co. (active 1896–1932)
Commercial firm

Based in Bombay, the firm Clifton & Co opened its studio in Meadows Street in 1896, the same year that cinema made its first appearance in India. Clifton & Co enthusiastically promoted this new medium, holding daily screenings at their studio throughout the following year. The studio is known primarily for documenting the transformation of Bombay into a large mercantile city. Some of these photographs were used in *The Bombay Presidency, The United Provinces, The Punjab, etc* by Somerset Playne (London, 1917–20), a survey of businesses across India. The company also sold photographs (and later postcards) of views covering the whole of India. In 1913 the firm moved from Meadows Street to Albert Buildings in Hornby Road, remaining there until the company's closure in 1932. In the mid-1890s, Clifton went into partnership briefly with a Mr Schultz in Bombay, as 'Schultz & Clifton'.

Dannenberg, John Christian A. *German* (d. 1905)
Commercial photographer

Dannenberg is first recorded as a daguerreotype artist in 1856 in Benares, although it is known that he spent some time in Lucknow before 1857 (see Ahmad Ali Khan). In 1858 Dannenberg's photographs were shown at the Bengal Photographic Society's annual exhibition. The following year Dannenberg became a member of the Society, and presented some of his views taken in Allahabad and Lucknow, documenting the aftermath of the Revolt. During the 1860s–70s Dannenberg moved around northern India, working principally in the hill stations: Landour (1862), Meerut (1865), Mussoorie (1865–69) and later in Aligarh (1871). In Meerut he entered into business with Middleton & Co. as a merchant. During this period he contributed ethnographical portraits to *The People of India* (1868–75, 8 volumes). By 1873 Dannenberg was living in Delhi, still working as a photographer, where between 1876 and 1880 he held the post of Sanitary Superintendent. In 1892 he marketed views of Lucknow and Cawnpore in a volume titled *Mutiny Memoirs*, which contained reprints of his own views of Lucknow alongside pirated copies of some of Beato's (q. v.) 1858–59 photographs.

Fitzgerald, Patrick Gerald *British* (1820–1910)
Amateur photographer

Employed in the Indian Medical Service between 1846 and 1879, Fitzgerald began his career as Assistant Surgeon with the Madras Artillery. Receiving promotions to Surgeon (1863) and Surgeon Major (1866), he finally achieved the post of Deputy Surgeon General of the Mysore Division (1875) before retiring in 1879. A keen amateur, he was one of the first photographers to reach Cawnpore after the fighting of 1857. In Lucknow from December 1857, Fitzgerald photographed the Alambagh and its surroundings, and made portraits of fellow officers of the Madras Fusiliers. Following the recapture of Lucknow in March 1858, Fitzgerald recorded the city's architecture before returning to Madras to pursue his medical career. He continued his enthusiasm for photography with a penchant for the well-posed group portrait, depicting social gatherings in Bangalore and Madras. Some of his views of Lucknow and Cawnpore were exhibited at the Madras Photographic Society's annual exhibition in December 1860.

Frith's Series (active 1870s–1971)
Commercial firm

The 'Frith's Series' photographs were printed by the British firm established by the photographer Francis Frith (1822–1898). Frith is primarily known for his three expeditions – to Egypt, Syria and Palestine – between 1856 and 1859, which resulted in the publication of seven books containing his own highly accomplished work. Frith also worked in Britain and Europe. The subsequent demand for his work was so great that Frith opened a printing establishment, under the name F. Frith & Co., in Reigate, Surrey. The firm was able to produce large quantities of albumen prints, and distribute photographs and stereoscopic views in albums and illustrated books. The company employed photographers in Britain to assemble a prodigious archive of views, which was complemented by the acquisition of other practitioners' work from around the world. During the 1860s Frith & Co. purchased the ethnographic work of William Johnson, previously published in *Indian Amateurs Photographic Album* (1856–58) and *Oriental Races and Tribes, Residents and Visitors of Bombay* (2 volumes, 1863–66). In 1875, a catalogue entitled *Frith's Universal Series* listed over four thousand photographs grouped by country or region. For India alone there was a choice of 1,445 photographs, recording all the major tourist sites, including twenty-three views of Lucknow.

La Grange, Baron Alexis Aimé de *French* (1825–1917)
Amateur photographer

A French aristocrat, La Grange was one of the earliest European photographers to arrive in India. He left Paris for India in 1849, accompanied by an older cousin, Félix Lambrecht (1819–1871). Initially planned for a period of four years, their expedition ended after only two years in 1851. La Grange and Lambrecht travelled mainly in northern India, but spent the last seven months of their journey in Ceylon, Java, and Singapore. En route to the subcontinent, La Grange encountered the French photographer Maxime du Camp in Egypt to whom he demonstrated Louis Désiré Blanquart-Evrard's adaptation of the calotype process. Between 1849 and 1851 La Grange visited several cities in northern India, including Benares, Dig, Fatehpur Sikri, Agra, Delhi and Lucknow; various towns in present-day Rajasthan, including Udaipur, Jaipur and Ajmer; and finally the caves at Ellora and Ajanta. Following his return to France La Grange compiled at least two important photographic albums illustrating Indian architecture. The first of these, containing sixty-one prints and entitled *Souvenirs de l'Inde anglaise*, was offered to Adolphe Thiers, the French statesman, journalist and historian. The second volume, *Photographies de l'Inde anglaise*, includes forty-eight architectural views. Both albums are now in public collections in Paris and Montreal respectively. After 1851 La Grange seems to have stopped photographing. Some of his views were reproduced in an album compiled by Victor Regnault in 1851, and five photographs were reproduced in Blanquart-Evrard's publication *L'Album photographique de l'artiste et de l'amateur* (1851). La Grange seems to have concentrated mainly on architectural views while in India. His two-part panorama made in Lucknow in 1849–51, illustrating the west face of the Rumi Darwaza and the surrounding area, is probably the earliest surviving photograph of Lucknow.

Lawrie & Co., G. W. *British* (active 1880–1920)
Commercial firm

Lawrie began his photographic career in 1880 in Nainital, working with established photographer John Edward Saché (q. v.) as Saché & Lawrie. The partnership was dissolved after only a couple of years when Lawrie set up an independent studio in Nainital. A second studio was opened in Lucknow in 1882 and the firm quickly became the most eminent photographic studio in the city. Lawrie expanded his business further with branches in Mussoorie (1890–94), Allahabad (1892–94), Bareilly (1895–1908) and Ranikhet (1895–1915). In later years the firm moved into book publishing, using the Lawrie & Co. photographs as illustrations. Postcards were also published from the early 1900s.

In 1903, the firm Lawrie & Co. was present at the Delhi Durbar to record the festivities.

Lyon, Captain Edmund David *Irish* (1825–1891)
Commercial photographer

In the British Army from 1845, Lyon abandoned his military career in 1854. After some time in Dublin, Lyon came to India c. 1862, making a photographic tour in northern India, including Agra, Delhi, Lucknow, Cawnpore and Dharamsala. The last series of views was completed 'at the express desire of Lady Elgin', as Dharamsala was the burial place of her late husband Lord Elgin, viceroy of India 1862–63. Between 1865 and 1869 Lyon ran a commercial studio in Ootacamund, concentrating on views of southern India. His coverage of the Nilgiris was presented at the Paris Universal Exhibition of 1867. Lyon was also commissioned by the governments of Madras and Bombay to photograph the archaeological antiquities and architecture of South India in 1867–68. His work was later acquired for the Archaeological Survey of India. His South Indian views were shown at the London Photographic Society Exhibition in 1869 and at the Exhibition of the Photographic Association, Cleveland, USA the following year, receiving high praise on both occasions. In 1873 he displayed a large number of prints at the Vienna Universal Exhibition, which were received with the same enthusiasm. Lyon left India in 1869 for England, stopping to photograph Malta. He later returned to settle in Malta in the late 1880s. Lyon also published two novels, *The Signora – a novel* (Remington & Co., London, 1883) and *Ireland's Dream: a romance of the future* (Sonnenschein & Co., London, 1888).

Macfarlane, Donald Horne *Scottish* (1830–1904)
Amateur photographer

Macfarlane arrived in India in 1859, as a partner in the firm Begg, Dunlop & Co., agents for tea and coal companies. Ini-

tially based in Cawnpore, Macfarlane seems to have spent much of his time at the firm's headquarters in Calcutta, or travelling in Darjeeling, Madras and the Nilgiri Hills, where he practised photography. In November 1860 he was elected a member of the Bengal Photographic Society, when he also presented a collection of recent views taken in Lucknow, Calcutta and north-west India. Initially interested by large-scale landscape photography, he also took portraits and stereoscopic photographs. In July 1861, exhibiting at the Fourth Annual Exhibition of the Bengal Photographic Society, he received the gold medal for the best landscape series and the silver for the best single photograph. By mid-1862 Macfarlane had been nominated vice-president of the Bengal Photographic Society, and continued to win gold and silver medals, including a prize for the best single photograph taken in India. In 1863 he became the president of the Society, and during the same year seconded Samuel Bourne (q. v.) for membership of the Society. At the beginning of the following year Macfarlane resigned from the Society, as his return to Britain was imminent. Shortly after his arrival home he joined the Photographic Society of London and received an award for his Indian views at the Society's 1864 exhibition. Macfarlane continued to photograph until his death in 1904, but seems to have exhibited his work for the last time at an exhibition in 1889, organized by the Photographic Society of Great Britain. To date, none of his photographs taken outside India has been identified. Macfarlane became a Member of Parliament for County Carlow (1880–85) and Argyllshire (1885–86 and 1892–95). He was knighted in 1894.

Milliken, John *British* (active late 1850s)
Amateur photographer

John Milliken was employed by the 23rd Company of Royal Engineers, initially as corporal and later promoted to captain. In August 1857 Milliken was in Sitapur, about fifty miles north of Lucknow, where he photographed the encampment of the Bengal Engineers. Between March and April 1858 Milliken was in Lucknow, being one of the first Europeans to record the aftermath of the Uprising of 1857. He photographed the Bara Imambara showing the breach in the surrounding walls, La Martinière with military camps in the foreground, Sikander Bagh, Musa Bagh with military personnel on the front steps, and Dilkusha Kothi. In early 1858 some of his photographs, including views of Singapore, were presented at the Exhibition of Photographs held at the South Kensington Museum, London.

Mushkoor-ud-Dowlah (Mushkoorooddowlah) *Indian*
(active 1860s)
Commercial photographer

In the 1860s Mushkoor-ud-Dowlah became a well-known commercial photographer in Lucknow, working for some time with his brother Asghar Jan (q. v.). While much of his work seems to have consisted of studio portraiture, some of his photographs held by the Lucknow State Museum include views of Qaisarbagh and the Shah Najaf Imambara, dated 1867. Mushkoor-ud-Dowlah was highly praised by P. C. Mookherjee in 1883: 'Mushkoor-ud-dowlah was the famous photographer of Lucknow and Oudh. His figures and views are excellent. He had an evenness of tone which common photographers cannot attain.'

Saché, John Edward *probably Prussian* (1824–1882)
Commercial photographer

Travelling from the United States, Saché arrived in Calcutta in late 1864. He entered into partnership with W. F. Westfield in 1865, based at 15 Waterloo Street, and became a member of the Bengal Photographic Society. The same year, the firm Saché & Westfield won the Silver Medal for the second best series of 'at least 10 photographs' at the annual exhibition of the Society. The firm was also commissioned by the Asiatic Society of Bengal to photograph a group of Andamanese people, who had been brought by a Mr Homfray to Calcutta as part of an ethnographical study. In 1866

Saché & Westfield received the bronze medal at the annual exhibition of the Bengal Photographic Society. In 1869 the firm was to incorporate the negative stock of the firm F. W. Baker & Co. into its catalogue. While remaining in partnership with Westfield, Saché opened his own independent studio at Nainital in 1867. Saché subsequently went into partnership (in 1868) with a Mr J. Murray for a short period, with a studio on Rampart Row in Bombay. Together they produced some unusual views of the Marble Rocks at Jabalpur. The same year Saché made an expedition into the Himalayas, trekking through to Pir Panjal glacier. By 1870 Saché had ended his partnership with Westfield and concentrated on his business in Nainital. He travelled extensively throughout northern India, photographing in all major towns and cities. The Lucknow studio was opened in 1871, although some of the Lucknow views appear to have been made before this date. In 1873–74 Saché made a series of views in Kashmir, which was to be the last group of topographical images he produced. Between 1874 and 1876, seasonally operating studios were opened in Meerut, Cawnpore and Benares. Saché started another branch of his business in 1876 in Mussoorie and continued to manage it, along with the studios at Nainital and Lucknow, until his death in 1882. A number of talented photographers worked in Saché's studios in the early years of their careers, including G. W. Lawrie (q.v.). During his twenty years in India, Saché produced a large number of accomplished photographs, proving himself a master of the picturesque composition.

Shepherd & Robertson *British* (active 1862–63)
Commercial firm

Charles Shepherd was already a well-known photographer in the mid-1850s, as in May 1858 he was asked to assist Robert Tytler (q. v.) in making some portraits of Abu'l-Muzaffar Siraj-ud-din Muhammad Bahadur Shah II, the last Mughal Emperor and his sons. Shepherd subsequently established a partnership in 1862 with Mr Arthur Robertson, as quoted in the trade inventory the *New Calcutta Directory*, which was to last for two years. Initially based in Agra, they transferred their studio in 1863 to Simla. During their partnership, Shepherd & Robertson produced an important collection of topographical views, covering Lucknow, Delhi, Agra, Fatehpur Sikri and Mussoorie. In addition they produced a series of ethnographical studies, some of which were used in *The People of India* (1868–75, 8 volumes). The Shepherd & Robertson partnership was dissolved when Shepherd went to work with Samuel Bourne (q. v.). A number of the Shepherd & Robertson photographs were incorporated into the Bourne & Shepherd catalogue, including the views of Lucknow.

Tytler, Robert Christopher *British* (1818–1872) and
Harriet Christina *British* (1828–1907)
Amateur photographers

Robert Tytler joined the Bengal Army in 1834 and participated in several conflicts, including the First Afghan War (1839–42) and the First Sikh War (1845–46). He was subsequently present at the 'Siege of Delhi', and the retaking of the city in September 1857. His wife Harriet was one of the few women present at the siege, as she could not leave the city owing to the advanced stage of her pregnancy. Following the conflict, Tytler was taught photography by Felice Beato (q. v.) and Dr John Murray (1809–1898), an amateur photographer based in Agra. He took up photography in order to assist his wife in the painting of a panorama of the Red Fort, Delhi. For six months in 1858, Robert and Harriet travelled extensively in northern India, visiting places affected by the recent Revolt, including Delhi, Meerut, Lucknow, Cawnpore, Agra and Benares. They took over 500 large-format paper negatives. Harriet also played an active role in the making of their photographs, by either assisting her husband or taking views herself. Some of the Tytlers' views appear to be very similar to photographs taken by Beato and Murray, and it seems likely that the couple accompanied them on photographic expeditions. Exhibited at the Photographic Society of Bengal in 1859, the negatives were praised as 'perhaps the finest series that has ever been exhibited to the Society' and in 1860, the Tytlers were awarded the gold medal for the best series of ten landscape photographs. Robert Tytler was made superintendent of the convict settlement at Port Blair in the Andaman Islands from 1862–64, and in 1865 transferred to Simla to be in charge of the museum, where he remained until his death in 1872. The Tytlers do not appear to have taken any photographs after their 1858 series.

THE BUILDINGS OF LUCKNOW

Alam Bagh (Garden of the World), house built by Wajid Ali Shah as a country retreat, to the south of Lucknow, c. 1850. Ruinous condition.

Asafi Kothi (House of Asaf [-ud-daula]). Attributed to a European designer, c. 1789. The chief building within the Daulat Khana palace complex. Extant.

Asafi Mosque (Mosque of Asaf [-ud-daula]), in the Bara Imambara complex, built 1784. Under British control from 1858 until 1884. Extant.

Aurangzeb Mosque, a late seventeenth-century mosque constructed during the reign of Emperor Aurangzeb on the Lakshman Tila mound, close to the Bara Imambara. Extant.

Baillie Guard Gate, the main entrance to the Residency, built 1814–15 by the British Resident John Baillie. Extant.

Banks' Bungalow, also called Hayat Bakhsh Kothi and now Raj Bhawan (Government House). Named Banks' Bungalow after John Sherbroke Banks, Chief Commissioner of Lucknow. Believed to incorporate Claude Martin's arsenal or powder mill, pre-1800. Extant, good condition.

Ba'oli, an elaborate step well, with interlinking passages leading off the courtyard of the Bara Imambara. Contains subterranean apartments used during the hot weather. Built by Shuja-ud-daula, 1760s. Extant.

Bara Chattar Manzil (Great Parasol Palace), the chief building in the Chattar Manzil palace complex, on the banks of the Gomti. Started c. 1803 by Saadat Ali Khan. Extant.

Bara Imambara (Great Imambara), also called the Asafi Imambara, built by Kifayut-ullah (by tradition a Persian architect) for Asaf-ud-daula, 1784–91. The complex includes the Asafi Mosque and the Ba'oli. Extant.

Barowen, also known as Baronne, and as Musa Bagh (Moses' Garden, or according to some, Monsieur's Garden). A country house built by Saadat Ali Khan, possibly from a design by Claude Martin, c. 1798. It bears similarities to the central portion of Government House in Calcutta. Ruinous condition.

Begum Kothi (Lady's House), on Hazratganj. Built by Amjad Ali Shah in 1844. Demolished 1980s.

Begum Kothi (Lady's House), part of the Residency complex. Late eighteenth-century building, at one time a European shop and in 1837–40 the home of Emma Walters, also known as the Welayti Begum. It now includes a small imambara (known as Sharaf-un-nissan) with graves and a mosque, added after 1840. Extant, ruinous condition.

Bibiapur Kothi, late eighteenth-century house, attributed to Claude Martin. Extant, ruinous condition.

Chattar Manzil (Parasol Palace), built around Lakh-e-pera. Begun c. 1803 and the chief nawabi palace until the completion of Qaisarbagh palace in 1852. Incorporates a number of separate houses including the Bara Chattar Manzil and the Darshan Bilas. Partially extant.

Chaulakhi Kothi (Four Lakh House), built by Azimullah Khan c. 1840, incorporated into Qaisarbagh palace. Demolished 1858.

Chaurukhi Kothi see Darshan Bilas.

Chaupar Stables (Fourway Stables), early nineteenth century, built by Saadat Ali Khan, off Hazratganj. Cruciform shape, only one 'arm' extant today, used as a social club.

Chini Bagh/Chini Bagh Gateway, leading to Chini Bazaar, once part of Qaisarbagh (q.v.). Named from the Chinese/china goods sold there. Bazaar demolished post c. 1870, but the gateway is partially extant.

Chota Chattar Manzil (Lesser Parasol Palace), part of the Chattar Manzil palace complex, begun by Saadat Ali Khan. Collapsed c. 1970.

Chota Imambara see Sibtainabad Imambara.

Christ Church, situated at the end of Hazratganj, built in 1860 as a memorial to those British who died in the Revolt of 1857. Designed by General Hutchinson, it was renovated in 1904. Extant, in good condition.

Constantia Claude Martin's country house, sometimes known as 'new Lakh-e-pera'. Designed and built by Martin, started in 1796, substantial additions made between 1840 and 1844 when it became the central portion of La Martin-ière College for Boys. Houses the tomb of General Martin in the basement. Extant.

Darshan Bilas (Delightful Aspect), also known as Chaurukhi Kothi (House of Four Faces). A separate building standing within the Chattar Manzil palace complex. Extant.

Daulat Khana (House of Wealth), built for Asaf-ud-daula, c. 1789, as the second nawabi palace complex. Included a number of separate buildings, tanks and gardens, including the Asafi Kothi. Largely demolished post-1858.

Dilaram Kothi (Heart's Ease House), stood on the north bank of the river, opposite the Chattar Manzil palace. Built either by Saadat Ali Khan as part of the new palace complex, or by his successor Ghazi-ud-din Haider. Demolished c. 1917.

Dilkusha Kothi (Heart-pleasing House), designed by Gore Ouseley for Saadat Ali Khan, c. 1805. Survives in a ruined condition.

Fairy Bridge (also known as the Merman Bridge) in Qaisarbagh palace. Partially extant.

Farhat Bakhsh (Felicity-bestowing), the new name given to Lakh-e-pera (a lakh of trees), Claude Martin's town house, after it was purchased by Saadat Ali Khan in 1803. Designed by Martin and completed in 1781, it subsequently became part of Chattar Manzil palace. Extant.

Gend Khana (Ball Court), a racquet court near the Husainabad Imambara, demolished c. 1860.

Gol Kothi (Round House), one of the separate European-style houses within the Daulat Khana palace complex. Built c. 1789. Demolished in the 1990s.

Gulistan-i-Iram (Rose Garden of Paradise), a separate building standing within the Chattar Manzil palace complex, started by Saadat Ali Khan, c. 1803. Extant.

Hayat Bakhsh Kothi see Banks' Bungalow.

Hazratganj, the main street of nawabi Lucknow, running east–west, south of the Gomti river. Built by Saadat Ali Khan. Extant.

Husainabad Imambara, built by Muhammad Ali Shah in 1837–78, now housing his tomb. Black-and-white building with courtyard, containing a small tank. Its eastern *tripolia* gateway stands in a direct line with Rumi Darwaza, which it resembles. Sometimes erroneously described as the Chota Imambara. Extant, in good condition.

Iron Bridge, a three-span bridge, commissioned by Saadat Ali Khan in 1810, designed by John Rennie, and made in England. Erected 1845, demolished in the 1950s.

Jal Pari, 'water fairy' gates, also known as the Mermaid Gateways. Part of Qaisarbagh (q.v.). A series of three gateways demolished c. 1870.

Jama Masjid (Friday or Congregational Mosque), started by Muhammad Ali Shah, in Husainabad, completed after his death by his widow Malika Jahan in 1845. The minarets collapsed in an earthquake c. 1890. Extant.

Jilau Khana (courtyard), sometimes an ante-chamber to a building. All four palace complexes in Lucknow contained at least one *jilau khana*. The term is most commonly encountered in connection with the central courtyard of the Qaisarbagh.

Kankarwali Kothi (Pebble House), built by Saadat Ali Khan on Hazratganj. Demolished after 1940.

Kazmain (or Karbala Kazmain/Rauza Kazmain), built in 1854 by the merchant Sharaf-ud-daula, and named after the town of Kazmain, in Iraq where the 7th Imam Musa Kazim is buried. Includes the tomb of Sharaf-ud-daula (d. 1863). Extant.

Khurshid Manzil (House of the Sun), also known as 'the Nawab's New House', designed and built by Captain Duncan McLeod for Saadat Ali Khan, and subsequently altered. Extant, in good condition, now La Martinière College for Girls.

La Martinière College, see Constantia and Khurshid Manzil.

Lakh-e-pera, see Farhat Bakhsh.

Lal Barahdari (Red Pavilion), also known as Qasrul Khakan (King's House), built for Saadat Ali Khan as the Durbar Hall. Converted to the Coronation Hall and Throne Room by Ghazi-ud-din Haider when he became king in 1819. Extant.

Lanka (bridge), an architectural folly that stood in Qaisarbagh Palace. Demolished c. 1911, replaced by the Amir-ud-daula Public Library.

Latkan Darwaza (Pendulum Gateway), so called from the large clock above the arch. Possibly built by Ghazi-ud-din Haider, in response to the Baillie Guard Gateway. Stood at the western end of Chattar Manzil palace, opposite the Residency. Demolished 1858.

Macchi Bhawan (House of the Fish), known both as a palace and a fort. A medieval fort, extensively embellished by Shuja-ud-daula, who built the Panch Mahalla pavilion within its walls. Partially demolished in 1857, and had disappeared by 1890. The King George and Queen Mary's Hospital and College stands on the site today.

Moti Mahal Palace (Pearl Palace), built by Ghazi-ud-din Haider. Partially extant.

Musa Bagh see Barowen.

Nur Bakhsh Kothi (Light-bestowing House), on Hazratganj, built by Saadat Ali Khan (r. 1798–1814). Extant.

Padshah Bagh (Emperor's Garden), a garden palace laid out by Nasir-ud-din Haider on north bank of the river Gomti. Lucknow University now stands here, but the ornamental canal and one pavilion remain. Partially extant.

Panch Mahalla (Five-storeyed Pavilion), within the Macchi Bhawan, built by Shuja-ud-daula. Probably lost in alterations made by his son Asaf-ud-daula.

Panch Mahalla Gateway, attributed to Shuja-ud-daula, c. 1764, stood at the entrance to the courtyard of the Panch Mahalla Pavilion. Demolished by 1890.

Picture Gallery, a red-coloured nawabi building, located near the Husainabad Imambara. Possibly part of the Daulat Khana palace, built by Asaf-ud-daula c. 1789. Its broad veranda may have been used as a viewing platform for entertainments and animal fights. Extant, fair condition.

Qadam Rasul (Footprint of the Prophet), small structure that housed an imprint of the Prophet Muhammad's foot, the imprint stone being lost during the Revolt of 1857. Built on an artificial mound near Shah Najaf, early nineteenth century. Extant, ruinous condition.

Qaisarbagh (Caesar's Garden), palace complex built between 1848 and 1852 (attributed to Ahmad Ali Khan) for Wajid Ali Shah. Its great courtyards enclosed several buildings including the Lanka, the Safaid Barahdari (the Taluqdars' Hall) and the Fairy Bridge. Partially extant.

Qaisarpasand see Roshan-ud-daula Kothi.

Qaisarbagh tombs, two monumental tombs, of Saadat Ali Khan and his wife Khurshid Zadi Begum respectively, at the northern end of the Qaisarbagh palace complex, c. 1815. Extant, fair condition.

Residency, a large complex containing many separate buildings. Home to the British Resident to the nawabi court and East India Company officials from 1775 to 1857. Besieged for six months during the Revolt of 1857. Preserved today as ruins.

Roshan-ud-daula Kothi or Kacheri (Court), built by Ghazi-ud-din Haider's chief minister, Roshan-ud-daula, 1827–37. Later renamed Qaisarpasand (Caesar's Pleasure). Partially extant.

Rumi Darwaza (Constantinople Gate), the western gateway of the great forecourt to the Bara Imambara. Attributed to Kifay-at-ullah, for Asaf-ud-daula, 1784. Designed to complement the existing Eastern Gateway of the Macchi Bhawan. Extant.

Safaid Barahdari (White Pavilion), also known as Qazrul Asa (House of Mourning) and today as the Taluqdars' Hall. The central building in the main courtyard of Qaisarbagh palace, originally built as an imambara by Wajid Ali Shah, between 1848 and 1852. Extant.

St Joseph's Church, the Catholic Church on Hazratganj. Built c. 1860, demolished 1980.

St Mary's Church, Anglican church, in the Residency. Built about 1845, mainly demolished in 1858.

Sangi Dalan (Stone Hall) within the Macchi Bhawan, built by Asaf-ud-daula, pre-1789. Date of demolition unknown.

Sat Khande (Seven-storeyed) tower, also known as 'Sat-khanda/Naukhanda' (Seven storeyed/nine storeyed). In fact only four storeys were built by Muhammad Ali Shah, with alternating Islamic and European façades. Extant.

Shah Najaf, an imambara, also known as Najaf Ashraf (the Noble Najaf), built by Ghazi-ud-din Haider, containing his tomb and the tombs of three wives. Extant, good condition.

Sharaf-un-nissan Imambara, a small imambara attached to the Begum Kothi in the Residency complex, (q.v.). Built by Sharaf-un-nissan, sister to Emma Walters (Welayti Begum), c. 1840. Extant.

Sher Darwaza (Lion Gateway), also called Neill's Gateway, standing north of Qaisarbagh. Extant.

Sibtainabad Imambara, on Hazratganj, commissioned by Amjad Ali Shah and includes his tomb. 'Sibtain' means grandsons, here referring to the grandsons of the Prophet, Hasan and Husain. Often referred to as Chota Imambara (Small Imambara). Used as a church by the British in 1858–60. Extant, some recent restoration.

Sikanderbagh (Sikander's Garden), a walled garden, containing a small house and mosque, built by Nawab Wajid Ali Shah for his wife Sikander Begum. Partially extant.

Stone Bridge, built, probably mid-1770s, by Asaf-ud-daula. Demolished c. 1912.

Taronwali Kothi (House of Stars), the royal observatory, begun by Captain James Herbert, astronomer, in 1832, completed by Lt. Col. R. Wilcox in 1840. Now the State Bank of India. Extant.

Tomb of Zinat Algiya, constructed c. 1838 for the daughter of Muhammad Ali Shah. It stands within the Husainabad Imambara complex adjacent to a mosque. Opposite is the *jawab*, an architectural 'answer' to the tomb, created to provide symmetry within the complex. Extant.

Zahur Bakhsh, a *kothi* constructed during the reign of Saadat Ali Khan, situated on Hazratganj.

THE NAWABS OF AWADH, 1722–1856

Saadat Khan
Burhan-ul-mulk
1722–1739

Safdar Jung
(nephew of Saadat Khan)
1739–1754

Shuja-ud-daula
(son of Safdar Jung)
1754–1775

Asaf-ud-daula
(son of Shuja-ud-daula)
1775–1797

Wazir Ali
(son of Asaf-ud-daula)
1797–1798

Saadat Ali Khan
(half brother of Asaf-ud-daula)
1798–1814

Ghazi-ud-din Haider
(son of Saadat Ali Khan)
1814–1827
Received title of
'King of Awadh' in 1819

Nasir-ud-din Haider
(son of Ghazi-ud-din Haider)
1827–1837

Muhammad Ali Shah
(brother of
Ghazi-ud-din Haider)
1837–1842

Amjad Ali Shah
(son of Muhammad Ali Shah)
1842–1847

Wajid Ali Shah
(son of Amjad Ali Shah)
1847–1856

NOTES

Introduction
Rosie Llewellyn-Jones

1   Modave 1971, p. 155.

2   Commissioned by the Governor General Warren Hastings, this painting shows the highly popular sport of cock fighting. This particular match has been arranged by Colonel John Mordaunt, the slim figure in white on the left of the painting. Mordaunt was a favourite of Nawab Asaf-ud-daula, the portly man who is gesturing towards him. In the top right is a self-portrait of the artist, Zoffany, with his elbow resting on his chair. Other individuals include Claude Martin who is seated on the sofa, with one leg crossed over the other.

3   Llewellyn-Jones 2000, p. 45.

4   See The Nawabs of Awadh, 1722–1856, pp. 259–61 of the present work.

5   The Dargah Hazrat Abbas, or Hazrat Abbas ka dargah, as it is also known, houses a banner of Abbas Ali, who was slain on the field of Karbala in AD 680. The *dargah* (shrine) is believed to have been built during Asaf-ud-daula's reign, but it was refurbished by Saadat Ali Khan, supposedly after a dream in which he saw the holy banner lying neglected.

6   Muhammad Ali Shah described the Husainabad Imambara as 'one of the most frequent places of Mahometan worship in this capital, and [it] has been built upon a scale of Magnificence suitable to the Power and Wealth of the Ruler of the Kingdom', a clear statement of how these grandiose religious buildings augmented the ruler's prestige. India Political Consultations, 22 May 1839, IOR.

7   India Public Consultations, 14 March 1845, no. 131, IOR.

8   Knighton 1865, p. 13.

9   Panoramas were popular in the mid-nineteenth century as photographers tried to imitate landscape paintings in the new medium. At the same time, the popularity of dioramas, with revolving painted scenes, was declining.

10 This series of thirty-four stereoscopic views can be accurately dated to March/April 1858, as the architectural evidence is identical to that seen in Felice Beato's photographs from the same period. Furthermore, the Indian men that appear in some of Beato's photographs also appear in a small number of these stereoscopic images in almost identical compositions, leading to the conclusion that these photographs were possibly taken by Beato, or by someone who was working alongside him.

11 The Orme Collection, MSS Eur Orme/334, Maps 9, 10 and 13, The British Library, London.

12 Oldenburg 1984, pp. 29–42.

13 The Diary of Ozias Humphry, 5 February to 19 June 1786. MSS Eur Photo 043, The British Library, London.

14 Llewellyn-Jones 2003b, p. 173.

15 See the long correspondence between the artist and the East India Company in 'The Cases of Ozias Humphry and James Paull', Add. 13532, The British Library, London.

16 See Ballerini 2003.

17 The location of these photographs, the position from which they were taken and the time of day they were taken have kindly been established for this book by Professor P. C. Little of Lucknow. The buildings stood at the south-west end of Hazratganj, just after the junction with the present-day Vidhan Sabha Marg. Fig. 94 was taken from somewhere near the present-day police station, probably during the summer, at about midday,

which would explain the emptiness of the scene in the extreme heat. Fig. 93 shows the Hazratganj studio of the photographer John Edward Saché, with his board affixed. This picture was taken during the winter, at about 11 am. 'Some three blocks away', Professor Little adds, 'we can also see part of a nawabi structure's battlement top, which could be the entrance to the Begum Kothi (Hazratganj); the presence of a full-loaded bullock cart in the middle of the road, as well as a tree-grove and crowd on the right may represent what was referred to as "a grain market or ganj" opposite the Begum Kothi post office in early Lucknow guide-books.' The Nowrojee family of Lucknow still own the estate shown in this photograph.

18 St Joseph's Church, which contained memorials to those killed in the Revolt of 1857, was demolished in the 1980s and a grandiose modern church erected in its place.

19 Ozias Humphry, *Claude Martin's Town House (later the Farhad Baksh) and the River Gomti*, pencil drawing, 5 May 1786. Add. 15965/plate i, The British Library, London.

Chapter 1: The Royal Palaces
Sophie Gordon

1 Fergusson 1910, p. 326.

2 The name Macchi Bhawan means 'Palace of the Fish', and is probably a reference to the nawabi motif of a fish, or more commonly, a pair of fishes. This motif derives from the title of *mahi maratib* ('Honour of the Fish') which was bestowed by Mughal emperors on particular noblemen. An alternative explanation is that the name was borrowed from Agra fort, where one of the main courtyards is known as Macchi Bhawan.

3 The Qudsia Bagh Palace and Garden was situated at the edge of the River Jumna, just north of Shahjahanabad. An aquatint by Thomas and William Daniell indicates that there may have been some similarities between the Lucknow and Delhi palaces, but as the Qudsia Bagh buildings have disappeared (with the exception of a mosque) this is difficult to investigate further. Daniell 1795, plate 3.

4 The gateway was photographed in 1858 by Felice Beato, and in 1874 by Darogha Ubbas Alli. The only change in sixteen years was the loss of the two short turrets on top of the gateway, either side of the central arch. This gateway survived until the heavy floods of 1923, when it collapsed. It was photographed by M. M. Beg in 1923, still surrounded by water: see Photo 10/8(31), The British Library, London. Some other buildings in Moti Mahal Palace still survive today, but in a much altered form.

5 Sharar [1975] 1994, p. 72.

6 Tandan 2001, p. 245.

7 Thiriez 1998. This study takes nineteenth-century photographs that had hitherto been approached only as art objects and accepts them as historical documents, subjecting them to the same scrutiny as any other historical source, with a particular insistence on precise and accurate dating.

8 Tieffenthaler 1786, vol. 1, pp. 256–57. The original reads: 'Le principal édifice est sans contredit celui que l'on nomme le palais quintuple, situé à une petite distance du bord méridional du Goumati, sur un lieu élevé; construit en forme de château, muni de murs & de hautes tours. Il a une porte fort élevée, et une vaste avantcour, qui précéde un haut bâtiment porté par des arcades, arrangé pour y sonner du tambour.'

9 There was another gateway in Lucknow, known as the *naubat khana*, which is described as standing 'about sixty yards in front, and to the left of the Baillie Guard' (i. e. the entrance to the British Residency compound). Mecham 1858, plate 16.

10 Hodges made an oil painting of Macchi Bhawan and Aurangzeb Mosque, entitled *A View of the Palace of the Nabob Asoph ul Dowlah at Lucknow*, 1783, private collection. This was used as the basis for the engraving that appears in his *Travels in India during the Years 1780, 1781, 1872 and 1783* (London 1793). Several other artists produced very similar views, e. g. Plate 5 of Henry Salt's *24 Views in St. Helena, The Cape, India, Ceylon, Abyssinia and Egypt* (London, 1809).

11 Hodges 1793, p. 100.

12 Anon., 'An Account of Lucknow (from Gladwin's Asiatic Miscellany …)' in *Asiatic Annual Register for the Year 1800*, p. 98.

13 Annesley 1809, pp. 109–10.

14 Gubbins 1858, p. 28.

15 Taylor 1996, p. 200.

16 Tandan 2001, p. 76.

17 The role of Napier and the changes undergone by the city after 1858 are discussed in Oldenburg 1984.

18 Ubbas Alli 1874b, p. 49.

19 Führer 1891, p. 266.

20 Asher 1995, p. 93.

21 Llewellyn-Jones 1985, p. 181.

22 Ibid., p. 182.

23 Eden 1866, pp. 88–89. Emily Eden visited Lucknow in 1838.

24 William Hodges stayed in the Farhat Bakhsh during May and June 1783 while he was recovering from an illness. He made at least two views of Martin's house, which are known only as engravings, both published in 1790 in *The European Magazine and London Review*. There were two large oil paintings in the possession of Claude Martin at the time of his death, and it seems likely that they relate to these prints. See Stuebe 1979, p. 247.

25 Sharar [1975] 1994 attributes the water pavilions to the reign of Saadat Ali Khan.

26 Ubbas Alli 1874b, p. 56.

27 Ibid., p. 32.

28 Llewellyn-Jones 2000, p. 34.

29 This is confirmed by a note found in a photograph album in the British Library. A view of Bara Chattar Manzil, dated 1860, is described, 'after it had been repaired and beautified by HM Govt. in 1858', Photo 147/1(31), The British Library, London.

30 Ubbas Alli 1874b, p. 32.

31 An anonymous photograph in the British Library, taken c. 1858, also shows some of the mosques immediately adjacent to the Darshan Bilas before they were destroyed. Photo 147/1(40), The British Library, London.

32 Tandan 2001, p. 90.

33 Das 1999, p. 3.

34 Ahmad Ali Khan, also known as Chhote Miyan, is identified as the architect of both Qaisarbagh Palace and the Husainabad buildings by P. C. Mookherjee. He writes that 'local photography began to flourish from about 1850 when an Englishman of the military line came here. Chota Miya designer of the Hoseinabad and Kaiserbagh buildings acquired the art from him and practised it to great profit and pleasure'. Mookherjee 1883, p. 183. See also Gordon 2003.

35 Reproduced in Das 1999, pp. 8–9.

36 The firman issued by Wajid Ali Shah allocated the revenue from a group of villages for the upkeep of this particular imambara. A copy of the firman is in the possession of Nawab Jafar Mir Abdullah.

37 These original pavilions can be seen in photographs taken in 1858, as in an example by J. C. A. Dannenberg, Photo 147/1(28), The British Library, London.

38 W. H. Russell wrote, 'Most hideous, ludicrous and preposterous are the Hindoo statues in imitation of Italian subjects which here and there deck the pedestals in the gardens.' Russell 1860, pp. 337–38.

39 Canning College was founded in 1864, but the building in Qaisarbagh palace was not constructed until the 1870s. It was opened by Sir George Cooper on 15 November 1878.

40 Sharar [1975] 1994, p. 64.

41 Tandan 2001, p. 109.

42 Ubbas Alli 1874b, p. 29.

43 Sharar [1975] 1994, p. 64.

44 Another set of these curious spiral staircases can be seen in Felice Beato's photograph of the main entrance of Sikandarbagh, dated 1858.

45 Ubbas Alli 1874a, Preface. The book was published simultaneously in English and in Urdu. The photographs have been attributed to Ubbas Alli: 'Daroga Abbas Ali [*sic*] … is a promising and enterprising photographer of no mean merit. He has published some books with photo-illustrations, *viz.* "the Lucknow album" of 50 buildings in English, the Beauties of Lucknow, about 25 dancing girls of this city in Urdu ….' Mookherjee 1883, p. 183.

46 The arguments both for and against the Lucknow school of architecture are discussed at length by others

and do not need repeating here. A useful discussion on the interpretation of the late Awadhi style, and the temptation to associate a debased style with a debased character, can be found in Tillotson 1989.

47 See, for example, Archer 1968; Welch 1978, no. 186; and Bautze 1998, no. 63.

Felice Beato's Panorama of the Great Imambara, 1858
E. Alkazi

1 Russell 1860, vol. 1, pp. 253–54; 257; 333 and 335.
2 Russell 1877, p. 392.

Chapter 2: Monumental Grief
Peter Chelkowski

The author is grateful to the H. Kevorkian Fund for providing the field-work grant for this project. Thanks also go to W. Sypniewski for help with the architectural drawings.

1 Canetti 1978, p. 146.
2 Bal'ami 1958, vol. 4, pp. 70–71.
3 Ibn Kathir 1993, vol. 6, p. 243.
4 Korom and Chelkowski 1994, pp. 150–75.
5 Canetti 1978, p. 150.
6 ''Alam va 'alamat', *Encyclopaedia Iranica*, vol. 1, fascicle 7, pp. 785–91. For a detailed description of the Indian *alams*, see Naqvi 1982, pp. 12–16.
7 Chelkowski 2001, pp. 324–41.
8 Chelkowski 1985, pp. 18–30.
9 'Rawda-khwani', *Encyclopedia of Islam*, p. 465; 'Rauzah Khvani,' *Oxford Encyclopedia of the Modern Islamic World*, vol. 3, pp. 412–13.
10 'Husayniyah', *Oxford Encyclopedia of the Modern Islamic World*, vol. 2, pp. 153–55.
11 Chelkowski 1979.
12 Rizvi 1986, vol. 2, p. 286.

13 Coburn (1991, p. 153) describes the Durga festival thus: 'It is an exuberant time, marked in one form or another by virtually every household. Neighborhood associations vie with one another in constructing images of Durga slaying Mahisa, and the procession of these images to the riverbank, where they will be immersed at the festival's end, is extraordinary. In Varanasi, for instance, hundreds of small groups accompany their respective images. Each Durga is lavishly decorated, celebrated by musicians, from a single drummer to a Western style brass band.'
14 Shakeel Hossain, 'Ritual Architecture and Urbanity', a poster designed for the exhibition 'Ritual Ephemeral Architecture', GSFA Gallery, University of Pennsylvania, Philadelphia, September 1997.
15 Ali [1832] 1917, p. 18.
16 Naqi 1974, p. 128.
17 Rivzi 1986, p. 295.
18 Pinault 1992, p. 80.
19 Naqvi 1982, pp. 5–76.
20 Mohid ud-Din Zore, *Hyat-e Meer Momin*, Hyderabad, n. d., p. 46, cited in Naqvi 1982.
21 Das 1991, p. 31.
22 Cole 1988, p. 103.
23 Llewellyn-Jones 1985, p. 203.
24 Knighton 1921, p. 91.
25 Roberts 1837, p. 349.
26 Annesley 1809, p. 156.
27 Pemble 1977, p. 13.
28 Cole 1988, p. 103.
29 Annesley 1809, p. 157.
30 A very thorough description of the architecture of the Bara Imambara is to be found in Tandan 2001.
31 Ali [1832] 1917, p. 20.
32 Llewellyn-Jones 1985, p. 203.
33 Rizvi 1986. The gist of the News Bulletin is given in vol. 2, pp. 309–16.

Chapter 3: The 'Country Houses' of Lucknow
Neeta Das

1 Girouard 1978.
2 Archer 1985.
3 Dutton 1935.
4 Ackerman 1966, p. 34.
5 Llewellyn-Jones 1997, p. 57.
6 Ibid., p. 55.
7 Annesley 1809, vol. 1, p. 236.
8 Das 1998, p. 15.
9 Llewellyn-Jones 1985, p. 177.
10 Ibid., p. 184.
11 Hjortshoj 1979.
12 Knighton 1856, p. 2.
13 Hjortshoj 1979, p. 56.
14 Sharar [1975] 1994.
15 Das 1998, p. 21.
16 Llewellyn-Jones 1985, p. 221.
17 Ibid., p. 218.
18 Ibid., p. 167.
19 Knighton 1856, p. 18.
20 Llewellyn-Jones 1985, p. 168.
21 Knighton 1856, p. 42.
22 Ibid., pp. 20–21.
23 Annesley 1809, p. 146.
24 Knighton 1856, p. 11.
25 Tandan 2001, p. 110.
26 Das 1998, p. 57.

Chapter 4: The Residency and the River
Rosie Llewellyn-Jones

1 Tieffenthaler 1786, vol. 1, p. 256.
2 'Origins of the Residency – Extract of Governor Hastings' Report of his Transactions at Benares', 4 October 1773, Home Misc. Series no. 345, pp. 329–48, IOR.
3 Llewellyn-Jones 2003b, p. 309, where Martin states he was honoured to be appointed in the service of His Excellency Shuja-ud-daula.
4 See Llewellyn-Jones 1992, Chapter Three, for a discussion of Martin's houses.
5 Bengal Secret Consultations, 25 February 1779, IOR.
6 Bengal Public Consultations, 28 July 1778, IOR.
7 Bengal Secret Consultations, 18 February 1779, IOR.
8 Ibid.
9 Diary of Ozias Humphry from 5 February to 19 June 1786. MSS Eur Photo 043, The British Library, London.
10 See Dalrymple 2002, illustration opposite p. 116.
11 Llewellyn-Jones 1985. See Chapter Five, 'The Resident and the Residency', for a fuller discussion on this topic.
12 Foreign Political Consultations, 14 October 1831, nos 45–46, NAND.
13 Foreign Political Consultations, 24 March 1853, nos 45–49, NAND.
14 Bengal Political Consultations, 7 March 1815, no. 16, IOR.
15 Hoffmeister 1848, p. 251.
16 Gubbins 1858, p. 162.
17 The earliest part of the Residency, a rectangular structure, can be traced in today's ruins by a close examination of the remaining brickwork. The removal of most of the stucco plaster enables us to see how new walls were applied at right angles to the original building to form a new entrance. The eight arches on the east façade, some now blocked up, correspond to those in Sita Ram's painting. The well to the right of the picture still exists.
18 A useful comparison can be made between the Bibiapur House, illustrated in Chapter Three of this book (fig. 90), and the Banqueting Hall (fig. 116).
19 Anon 1858, p. 130.
20 Llewellyn-Jones 2000, pp. 152–55.
21 Keene 1896, p. 63.
22 Ubbas Alli 1874b, p. 45.
23 Archaeological Survey of India 1902/3, pp. 23–24.
24 See Hoey 1885.
25 Keene 1896, p. 51.
26 Tandan 2001, pp. 169–70.
27 Thomas and William Daniell A panoramic view of Lucknow, pencil, 1789. Reproduced in Spink 1996, no. 4, p. 8.

28 Foreign Political Consultations, 14 July 1810, no. 138, NAND.

29 Foreign Political Consultations, 29 February 1812, no. 70, NAND.

30 Heber 1828, vol. 1. p. 405.

31 Nugent 1839, vol. 1, p. 323.

32 Llewellyn-Jones 2000, pp. 70–72.

33 Ubbas Alli 1874b, p. 19.

34 Gubbins 1858, p. 390.

Chapter 5: La Martinière: An Enlightened Vision
Nina David

The original name given to Claude Martin's country house was Constantia. It became known as La Martinière after the establishment of the college for boys in the early 1840s.

1 Russell [1860] 1957, p. 56.

2 'Last Will and Testament of Cl. Martin', Article Thirty-two, p. 66.

3 Spear [1932] 1980, p. 133.

4 Claude Martin to Ozias Humphry, 11 March 1789. Letter in the Royal Academy, London.

5 Qureshi 2002, vol. 1, pp. 162–63.

6 Llewellyn-Jones 1992, pp. 203–4.

7 Andrews 1942, p. 6.

8 Unpublished English translation of contemporary Persian manuscript, 'Tarikh-e-Sa'adat', by Munshi Imam Baksh 'Bedaar', Chapters 29–51, Amir ud-daula Library, Lucknow. One of the best sources of information on the period of Nawab Saadat Ali Khan, it is written in the form of *saqi namah* ('wine server/cup bearer'). *Saqi namah* is a form of *masnavi* or Persian poetry in which a subject is described in a systematic manner – as when, at the end of each story, the poet addresses the *saqi* or wine server, requesting him/her to serve him more wine. Edited and translated by S. A. Zafar, Senior Reader, Department of Persian, Lucknow University, 2003.

9 Hill 1901, p. 72.

10 Bengal Wills, 1800, no. 41, IOR.

11 Saint Venant 1996, p. 58. Mme Marie-Gabrielle de Saint Venant, based in Paris, is a sixth-generation direct descendant of Benoît de Boigne and the keeper of the private archives of the Conte de Boigne. She stated to the author when they met, in 1997, that her ancestor Benoît de Boigne left India on 17 January 1797.

12 Annesley 1809, pp. 162–63

13 Heber 1849, vol. 1, p. 385.

14 Orlich 1845, vol. 2. p. 98.

15 Hill 1901, p. 27.

16 Keene 1896.

17 The building of Constantia had started by June 1796. See Llewellyn-Jones 2003b, p. 287.

18 Benett [1877–78] 1993, vol. 2, p. 360.

19 Author's interview with Mr Nur-ul Azeem, March 2002, Lucknow.

20 'Last Will and Testament of Cl. Martin', Article Twenty-seven, p. 52.

21 Bute 1828.

22 Report on Constantia prepared for INTACH, New Delhi, by Sanskriti Rawat, 1996, p. 30.

23 Ibid., p. 38.

24 Claude Martin to M. D'Aguiton, Calcutta, 22 August 1793. Private archives of the de Boigne family, Paris. Mme Marie-Gabrielle de Saint Venant is in charge of the private correspondence (written from Lucknow) between Claude Martin and General Benoît de Boigne (with a few additional letters from Claude Martin, including those to M. D'Aguiton). Mme de Saint Venant very kindly showed me the letters and said that I was the first person to see the originals, written in French on fine pale blue paper between January 1797 and February 1800. Most importantly, she firmly felt that copies of the letters must go back to the place from where they originated – Lucknow.

25 Claude Martin's Will names his seven mistresses as Boulone (known also as Lize), her two sisters Gomani and Animan, Sally (the illegitimate daughter of a former British Resident at Lucknow, Col. Gabriel Harper), Maria Daye, Kariman and Panna.

26 'Last Will and Testament of Cl. Martin', Article Thirty, p. 57.

27 Dalrymple 2002, p. 272.

28 Annesley 1809, vol. 1, p. 165.

29 Heber 1849, vol. 1, p. 385.

30 Bute 1828.

31 'Last Will and Testament of Cl. Martin', Article Thirty-one, p. 64.

32 Bhatnagar 1995, p. 18.

33 Foreign Political Index, 29 August 1838, NAND.

34 Foreign Political Index, 1 January 1840, NAND.

35 The Girls' School is housed in the Khurshid Manzil, formerly known as the '32nd Mess House', a large double-storeyed building on high ground. Initially more than Rs 100,000 was utilized from the Martinière 'Female Education Fund' for the establishment of a boarding school, which was formally approved by the Calcutta High Court in July 1869.

36 Foreign Political Index, 9 August 1841, Lieut. Cunningham's report for 1 October 1840 to 1 April 1841, NAND.

37 Ibid.

38 Foreign Political Index, Captain H. Fraser's report of 13 January 1844. NAND.

39 La Martinière Records, Lucknow, the Principal's report for 31 March 1879.

40 Jesse 1945.

41 La Martinière Records, Lucknow, the Principal, Mr T. G. Sykes' report for 1883. The report states that 'Like our own Robin Hood he [Claude Martin] gave to the poor', and mentions '... his solicitude that this building which he always calls his tomb, should be kept in good repair.'

42 La Martinière Records, Lucknow. The Principal's report for 1872, Item 39, states, 'In the garden nursery the following trees and ornamental shrubs, amounting to nearly thirteen thousand have been raised, and some two thousand planted out. The size of the young trees will not yet permit the park to be grazed.' Trees and plants included mango, lychee, tamarind, 'belatee neem', peepul, bamboo, lemon, cypress, roses and hibiscus.

43 Report on Constantia prepared for INTACH, New Delhi, by Sanskriti Rawat, 1996.

GLOSSARY

bagh – a garden

baoli – a step-well

barahdari – a square or rectangular, airy, pavilion-like building of one storey, and having at least twelve openings; often found in formal gardens, and used for entertainment

bazaar – a market

begum – respectful term for a married woman; a princess or lady of rank

bibi – an Indian wife, consort or long-term companion

charbagh – lit. a 'four garden' plan; a formal garden, the design originating in Persia, divided into four sections, or multiples of four, usually by water channels

chattri – lit. 'umbrella'; a small domed kiosk usually positioned on the corners of flat roofs

dargah – a Muslim shrine, usually the burial site of a saint or relic associated with him

darshan – the viewing or sight of an important or religious person, such as a Hindu deity, a ruler or a holy man

darwaza – a gateway

durbar – a royal court or gathering, presided over by a person of rank, from the Persian *darbar*

ganj – a market street lined with shops and usually closed at both ends with a gate

imambara – a building usually of one storey, used by Shias for mourning rituals during Muharram; a repository for *taziyas*, and sometimes a burial place for Shia rulers

jali – a perforated stone screen, often of marble or sandstone

jawab – lit. 'answer'; in an architectural context, it refers to a structure positioned as a symmetrical double

Karbala – the place in Iraq where the Prophet's grandsons were martyred and subsequently buried; in India the word describes a Shia shrine and cemetery

kothi – a large house, usually European style, without the traditional inner courtyard

lath – a monumental column or pillar

maidan – a large, grassy area, used for sports, horse-riding, outdoor meetings and walks

masjid – a mosque

Muharram – the annual month of mourning by Shias for the martyrs of Karbala

nawab – a ruler, derived from *naib*, the Persian word for deputy

qila – a fort

raj bhawan – lit. 'ruler's house', now the office of a state
    governor in India

serai – a temporary lodging house, used by travellers
    and pilgrims, with sleeping cells, and sometimes
    a courtyard for animals

shish mahal – lit. 'glass palace'; a room decorated with
    mirrors

sipahi – 'sepoy', an Indian soldier in the East India
    Company army or, later, in the British Indian Army

subahdar – a governor

talao – a lake or pool of water

taziya – a portable replica of the tombs of Husain and the
    Karbala martyrs, highly decorated and carried in
    procession during Muharram (India); the theatrical
    re-enactment of the martyrdom of Husain (Iraq)

tripolia – a three-arched gateway

tykhana – underground or semi-basement room, used
    for storage and shelter during the hot weather

zenana – the women's or private family quarters in
    a household

SELECT BIBLIOGRAPHY AND WORKS CITED

Abbreviations

INTACH: Indian National Trust for Art & Cultural
Heritage, New Delhi
IOR: India Office Records, at The British Library,
London
NAND: National Archives, New Delhi

A Journey Through India. Pictures of India by British Artists. Intr. Anthony Spink and Karen Taylor. London: Spink & Son, 1996.

Abbas, Syed Anwer. *Wailing Beauty: The Perishing Art of Nawabi Lucknow.* Lucknow: S. Anwer Abbas, 2002.

Ackerman, James. *Palladio.* Harmondsworth: Penguin, 1966.

Ali, Mrs Meer Hasan. *Observations on the Mussulmauns of India.* [First published London: Parbury Allen, 1832.] Reprinted London: Oxford University Press, 1917.

Allen, Charles. *A Glimpse of a Burning Plain: Leaves from the Indian Journal of Charlotte Canning.* London: Michael Joseph, 1986.

Andrews, W. E. *Major General Claude Martin, HEICS.* Lucknow: Lucknow Publishing House, 1942.

Annesley, George (later Viscount Valentia). *Voyages and Travels to India, Ceylon, the Red Sea, Abyssinia and Egypt in the years 1802, 1803, 1804, 1805 and 1806.* London: William Miller, 1809.

Anon. *A Lady's Diary of the Siege of Lucknow, written for the perusal of friends at home.* London: John Murray, 1858. Reprinted as Mrs G. Harris *A Lady's Diary of the Siege of Lucknow.* Delhi: Asian Educational Services, 1997.

Archaeological Survey of India Annual Report 1902/3. Calcutta: Superintendent of Government Printing, 1904.

Archer, John. *The Literature of British Domestic Architecture 1715–1842.* Cambridge, Mass.: MIT, 1985.

Archer, Mildred. 'Gardens of Delight'. *Apollo*, vol. 88, no. 79 (new series), September 1968, pp. 172–84.

Asher, C. *Architecture of Mughal India.* The New Cambridge History of India, vol. 1:4. New Delhi: Cambridge University Press, 1995.

The Asiatic Annual Register or a View of the History of Hindustan, and of the Politics, Commerce and Literature of Asia for the Year 1800. London, 1801.

Azadari : a historical review of institution of azadari for Imam Husain : translation of Aza-i-Husaini par tarikhi tabsera. Trans. Syed-Ali Naqi. Karachi: Peermahomed Ebrahim Trust, 1974.

Bal'ami, Abou 'Ali-Mo'hammed. *Chronique de Abou-Djafar Mo'hammed-ben-Djarir-ben Yezid Tabari.* Trans. Hermann Zotenberg. Paris, 1958.

Ballerini, Julia. 'Rites of Passage: A Frenchman's Albums of British India'. In *Traces of India. Photography, Architecture, and the Politics of Representation, 1850–1900.*

ed. M. A. Pelizzari. Montreal: Canadian Centre for Architecture and Yale Center for British Art, 2003, pp.86–105.

Bautze, J. *Interaction of Cultures: Indian and Western Painting 1780–1910*. Alexandria, Va., 1998.

Benett, William Charles, ed. *Gazetteer of the Province of Oudh*. [First published Allahabad: Oudh Government Press, 1877–78.] Reprinted Delhi: Low Price Publications, 1993.

Bhatnagar, G. D. *Awadh under Wajid Ali Shah*. Benares: Bharatiya Vidya Prakashan, 1968.

Bhatnagar, Satish. *Bright Renown: La Martinière College*. Lucknow: La Martinière College, 1995.

Blunt, Alison. 'Home and Empire: Photographs of British Families in the *Lucknow Album*, 1856–57'. In *Picturing Place: Photography and the Geographical Imagination*, ed. J. Ryan and J. Schwartz. London: I. B. Tauris, 2003, pp. 243–60.

Bute, Marchioness of, ed. *The Private Journals of the Marquess of Hastings*. London: Saunders and Otley, 1828.

Canetti, Elias. *Crowds and Power*. New York: The Seabury Press, 1978.

Chappell, W. 'Camera Vision at Lucknow'. *Image*, vol. 7, no. 2, February 1958, pp. 36–40.

Chelkowski, Peter, ed. *Ta'ziyeh: Ritual and Drama in Iran*. New York: New York University Press, 1979.

Chelkowski, Peter. 'Shia Muslim Processional Performances'. *The Drama Review*, vol. 29, no. 3, Fall 1985, pp. 18–30.

Chelkowski, Peter. 'Popular Religious Art in the Qajar Period'. In *The Splendour of Iran*, ed. N. Pourjavady, London: Booth-Clibborn Editions, 2001.

Coburn, Thomas B. *Encountering the Goddess*. Albany, N.Y.: SUNY Press, 1991.

Cole, Juan R. I. *Roots of North Indian Shi'ism in Iran and Iraq: Religion and State in Awadh 1722–1859*. Berkeley: University of California Press, 1988.

Dalrymple, William. *White Mughals: Love and Betrayal in Eighteenth Century India*. London: Harper Collins, 2002.

Daniell, Thomas. *Oriental Scenery. Twenty Four Views in Hindoostan taken in the years 1789 and 1790*. London: Robt. Bowyer, 1795.

Das, Neeta. *The Architecture of Imambaras*. Lucknow: Mahotsav Patrika Samiti, 1991.

Das, Neeta. *Indian Architecture: Problems in the Interpretation of 18th and 19th century Architecture. A Study of the Dilkusha Palace, Lucknow*. Delhi: B. R. Publishing Corporation, 1998.

Das, Neeta. *Kaiserbagh: The Garden Palace of Lucknow*. Lucknow: U. P. Tourism, 1999.

Das, Neeta. 'A Lost Pairidaeza Restored: Kaiserbagh, the garden palace, Lucknow'. *Architecture + Design*, vol. 17, no. 6, Nov.–Dec. 2000, pp. 120–24.

Dewan, Janet. 'The Private Life of an Eastern Photographer – Charles William Derusett of Simla'. In *History of Photography*, vol. 21, no.3, Autumn 1997, pp. 230–35.

Dutton, Ralph, Baron Sherborne. *The English Country House*. London: Batsford, 1935.

Eden, Emily. *'Up the Country': Letters written to her sister from the Upper Provinces of India*. London: Richard Bentley, 1866.

Encyclopaedia Iranica. Ed. Ehsan Yarshater. 11 vols to date. London: Routledge & Kegan Paul, 1982–.

Encyclopedia of Islam (New Edition). Ed. Th. Bianquis, C. Bosworth, E. van Danzel and W. P. Heinrichs. 11 vols. Leiden: Brill, 1986–2002.

Fayrer, Sir Joseph. *Recollections of my Life*. London: W. Blackwood & Sons, 1900.

Fergusson, James. *History of Indian and Eastern Architecture*. 2 vols. London: John Murray, 1910.

Fisher, Michael. *A Clash of Cultures: Awadh, the British and the Mughals*. New Delhi: Manohar Publications, 1987.

Führer, A. *The Monumental Antiquities and Inscriptions in the North Western Provinces and Oudh*. Archaeological Survey of India, Imperial Series, vol. 2. Allahabad: Government Printing Press, 1891.

Girouard, Mark. *Life in the English Country House: A Social and Architectural History*. New Haven: Yale University Press, 1978.

Gordon, Sophie. '"A Silent Eloquence": Photography in 19th Century Lucknow.' In Llewellyn-Jones 2003a, pp. 134–45.

Gubbins, Martin. *An Account of the Mutinies in Oudh and of the Siege of the Lucknow Residency*. London: Richard Bentley, 1858.

Hasan, Amir. *Palace Culture of Lucknow*. Delhi: BR Publishing Corporation, 1983.

Hay, Sidney. *Historic Lucknow*. [First published Lucknow: Pioneer Press, 1939.] Reprinted Delhi: Asian Educational Services, 1994.

Heber, Bishop Reginald. *Narrative of a journey through the upper provinces of India from Calcutta to Bombay, 1824–25 (with notes upon Ceylon), an account of a journey to Madras and the Southern Provinces, 1826, and letters written in India*. 3 vols. 2nd edition London, 1828. Reprinted (2 vols) London: John Murray, 1849.

Hill, S. C. *The Life of Claud Martin, Major General in the Army of the Honourable East India Company*. Calcutta: Thacker, Spink & Co., 1901.

Hilton, E. H. *Guide to Lucknow and Residency*. Lucknow: Lucknow Publishing House, 1934.

Hjortshoj, Keith. *Urban Structures and Transformations in Lucknow, India*. South Asia Occasional Papers and Theses No. 7, South Asia Program, Cornell University. Ithaca, N.Y.: Cornell University Press, 1979.

Hodges, William. *Travels in India during the Years 1780, 1781, 1782 and 1783*. London, 1793.

Hoey, William. *Tafzih u'l Ghafilin (The History of Asaf-ud-daula)*. Allahabad, 1885

Hoffmeister, Dr W. *Travels in Ceylon and Continental India; including Nepal and other parts of the Himalayas to the borders of Thibet. With some notices of the Overland Route*. Edinburgh, 1848.

Ibn Kathir. *Al-Bidaya wa al-Nihaya*. Ed. Editing Board of al-Turath. 15 vols. Beirut: Dar Ihya' al-Turath al-'Arabi, 1993.

Jesse, William. 'Martinière Reminiscences'. In *Constantia*, the magazine of La Martinière College, 1945.

Keene, H. G. *Keene's Handbook for Visitors to Allahabad, Cawnpore and Lucknow*. Calcutta: Thacker, Spink & Co., 1896.

Kidwai, R. R. *Lucknow: The Lost Paradise*. Lucknow: SR Publications, 1993.

Knighton, William. *Elihu Jan's Story, or the Private Life of an Eastern Queen*. London: Longman Green, 1865.
Knighton, William. *The Private Life of an Eastern King*. London: Routledge & Co, 1856. New edition ed. S. B. Smith, London: Oxford University Press, 1921.

Korom, Frank, and Peter Chelkowski. 'Community Process and the Performance of Muharram Observances in Trinidad'. *The Drama Review*, vol. 38, no. 2, Summer 1994, pp. 150–75.

Llewellyn-Jones, Rosie. *A Fatal Friendship: The Nawabs, the British and the City of Lucknow*. New Delhi: Oxford University Press, 1985.

Llewellyn-Jones, Rosie. *A Very Ingenious Man: Claude Martin in early Colonial India*. New Delhi: Oxford University Press, 1992.

Llewellyn-Jones, Rosie. 'The Courtly Style. The Remaking of Lucknow'. In *Victorian and Edwardian Architecture in India*, ed. C.W. London. Bombay: Marg Publications, 1994, pp. 74–84.

Llewellyn-Jones, Rosie. 'Lucknow, City of Dreams'. In *Lucknow: Memories of a City*, ed. Violette Graff. New Delhi: Oxford University Press, 1997, pp. 49–66.

Llewellyn-Jones, Rosie. *Engaging Scoundrels: True Tales of old Lucknow*. New Delhi: Oxford University Press, 2000.

Llewellyn-Jones, Rosie, ed. *Lucknow Then and Now*. Mumbai: Marg Publications, 2003a.

Llewellyn-Jones, Rosie. *A Man of the Enlightenment in 18th century India: Letters of Claude Martin*. New Delhi: Permanent Black, 2003b.

Martin, Claude. *The Last Will and Testament of the Major General Cl. Martin*. Lyon: De l'imprimerie de Ballanche père et fils, 1803.

Mecham C. H., and G. Couper. *Sketches & Incidents of the Siege of Lucknow from drawings made during the siege by Clifford Henry Meecham, with descriptive notices by George Couper*. London: Day & Son, 1858.

Menezes, Lt Gen. S. L. *Fidelity and Honour: The Indian Army from the 17th to the 21st Century*. New Delhi: Oxford University Press, 2001.

Modave, Comte de. *Voyage en Inde du Comte de Modave (1773–1776)*. Paris: Ecole française d'Extrême-Orient, 1971.

Mookherjee, P. C. *Pictorial Lucknow*. Lucknow: P. C. Mookherjee, 1883.

Naqvi, Sadiq. *Qutb Shahi 'Ashur Khanas of Hyderabad City*. Hyderabad: Bab-ul-Ilm Society, 1982.

Nevill, H. R., ed. *Lucknow: A Gazetteer*. District Gazetteers of the United Provinces of Agra and Oudh, vol. 37. Allahabad: Government Printing Press, 1904.

Nillson, Sten. *European Architecture in India*. New York: Taplinger, 1969.

Nugent, Lady Maria. *A Journal for the Year 1811 till the Year 1815*. 2 vols. London, 1839.

Oldenburg, Veena Talwar. *The Making of Colonial Lucknow 1856–1877*. Princeton, N. J.: Princeton University Press, 1984.

Orlich, Leopold von. *Travels in India, including Sinde and the Punjab*. Trans. H. Evans Lloyd. London, 1845.

Oxford Encyclopedia of the Modern Islamic World. Ed. John E. Esposito. New York: Oxford University Press, 1995.

Parks, Fanny. *Wanderings of a Pilgrim in Search of the Picturesque*. London: Pelham Richardson, 1828.

Pemble, John. *The Raj, the Indian Mutiny and the Kingdom of Oudh 1801–1859*. Hassocks: Harvester Press, 1977.
Pinault, David. *The Shiites: Ritual and Popular Piety in a Muslim Community*. London and New York: I. B. Tauris, 1992.

Praveen, Yogesh. *Lucknow Monuments*. Lucknow: Pnar Publications, 1989.

Qureshi, H. A. *The Flickers of an Independent Nawabi. Nawab Wazir Ali Khan of Awadh*. Lucknow: New Royal Book Company, 2002.

Rizvi, Saiyid Athar Abbas. *A Socio-Intellectual History of the Isna 'Ashari Shi'is*. 2 vols. New Delhi: Munshiram Manoharlal, 1986.

Roberts, Emma. *Scenes and Characteristics of Hindostan*. 2nd edition, 3 vols. London: W. H. Allen, 1837.

Russell, W. H. *My Diary in India in the Year 1858–59*. London, 1860. Republished as *My Indian Diary by William Howard Russell*, ed. Michael Edwardes, London: Cassell & Co., 1957.

Russell, W. H. *The Prince of Wales' Tour: A Diary in India, with some account of the visits of His Royal Highness to the courts of Greece, Egypt, Spain and Portugal*. London: Sampson Low, Marston, Searle & Rivington, 1877.

Saint Venant, Marie-Gabrielle de. *Benoît de Boigne (1751–1830): du général au particulier*. Mémoires et documents de la Société Savoisienne d'Histoire et d'Archéologie, vol. 98. Chambéry: Société Savoisienne d'Histoire et d'Archéologie, 1996.

Sharar, Abdul Halim. *Lucknow: The Last Phase of an Oriental Culture*. Trans. and ed. E. S. Harcourt and Fakhir Hussain. [First published London: Paul Elek, 1975.] Reprinted New Delhi: Oxford University Press, 1994.

Sharma, Brij Bhushan. 'Darogha Ubbas Alli: An Unknown 19th century Indian Photographer'. *History of Photography*, vol. 7, no. 1, January 1983, pp. 63–68.

Sinha, Amita. 'Decadence, Mourning and Revolution: Facets of the 19th century landscape of Lucknow, India'. *Landscape Research*, vol. 24, no. 2, pp. 123–36.

Sleeman, Maj. Gen. W. H. *A Journey through the Kingdom of Oudh in 1849 to 1850*. London: Richard Bentley, 1858.

Spear, Percival. *The Nabobs: A Study of the Social Life of the English in Eighteenth Century India*. [First published 1932.] Reprinted London: Curzon Press, 1980.

Stuebe, I. C. *The Life and Works of William Hodges*. New York: Garland, 1979.

Tandan, Banmali. *The Architecture of Lucknow and its Dependencies 1722–1856. A Descriptive Inventory and an Analysis of Nawabi Types*. New Delhi: Vikas Publishing House, 2001.

Taylor, P. J. O. *Chronicles of the Mutiny and other Historical Sketches*. New Delhi: Indus, 1992.

Taylor P. J. O. *A Companion to the 'Indian Mutiny' of 1857*. New Delhi: Oxford University Press, 1996.

Thiriez, Régine. *Barbarian Lens: Western Photographers of the Qianlong Emperor's European Palaces*. London: Gordon and Breach Publishers, 1998.

Tieffenthaler, Joseph. 'La Géographie de l'Indoustan'. In J. Bernouilli, *Description Historique et Géographique de l'Inde*. 3 vols. Berlin: Jean Bernouilli, 1786–89.

Tillotson, G. H. R. *The Tradition of Indian Architecture: Continuity, Controversy and Change since 1850*. New Haven: Yale University Press, 1989.

Ubbas Alli, Darogha (Darogah Abbas Ali). *The Beauties of Lucknow*. Calcutta: Calcutta Central Press Company Ltd, 1874a.

Ubbas Alli, Darogha (Darogah Abbas Ali). *The Lucknow Album, containing a series of fifty photographic views of Lucknow and its environs, etc.* Calcutta: G. H. Rouse, 1874b.

Welch, S. C. *Room for Wonder: Indian Painting during the British Period, 1760–1880*. New York: National Federation of Arts, 1978.

Cover photograph and Fig. 58: Clifton & Co., Asafi Mosque and Bara Imambara viewed from the Rumi Darwaza, photographer's ref. 1254, gelatin silver print, c. 1900, 238 x 287 mm.

Front Endpaper: Frith's Series, Chaulakhi Gateway, leading out of the Jilau Khana, Qaisarbagh, photographer's ref. 3047, albumen print, mid-1870s, 160 x 210 mm.

Fig. 1: Frith's Series, North-east Gate, Qaisarbagh, photographer's ref. 3046, albumen print, mid-1870s, 152 x 207 mm.

Fig. 4: Ahmad Ali Khan, working as 'Chhote Miyan', Bara Chattar Manzil, Farhat Bakhsh and adjacent palace building, albumen print, 1860, 183 x 273 mm.

Fig. 7: Edmund David Lyon, Shopkeeper, albumen print, c. 1862, 193 x 193 mm.

Fig. 10: John Edward Saché, North end of the Jilau Khana, Qaisarbagh, with the Tombs of Saadat Ali Khan and Begum Khurshid Zadi beyond, photographer's ref. 162, albumen print, c. 1867, 217 x 279 mm.

Fig. 15: Donald Horne Macfarlane,
Macchi Bhawan after restoration,
albumen print, c. 1860, 197 x 242 mm.

Fig. 18: Darogha Ubbas Alli, Gateway
to the Moti Mahal, Plate 16 from
The Lucknow Album, albumen print,
c. 1870, published 1874, 104 x 151 mm.

Fig. 19: Samuel Bourne, Looking west
towards the Chattar Manzil complex,
photographer's ref. 1018, albumen print,
December 1864–early 1865, 237 x 292 mm.

Fig. 20: J. C. A. Dannenberg,
Gulistan-i-Iram (left), Chota Chattar
Manzil (centre) and Darshan Bilas (right),
albumen print, c. 1860, 242 x 293 mm.

Fig. 21: Samuel Bourne,
Darshan Bilas and Chota Chattar Manzil,
photographer's ref. 1019, albumen print,
December 1864–early 1865, 226 x 292 mm.

Figs. 23 and 104: Felice Beato,
Dilkusha Kothi, photographer's ref. L 3,
albumen print, 1858, 255 x 306 mm.

Figs. 25 and 101: Felice Beato, Barowen,
also known as Musa Bagh,
albumen print, 1858, 252 x 303 mm.

Fig. 26: John Edward Saché, Lal Barahdari,
photographer's ref. 198, albumen print,
c. 1867, 230 x 287 mm.

Fig. 27: John Edward Saché, Chota
Chattar Manzil, photographer's ref. 195,
albumen print, c. 1867, 232 x 288 mm.

Fig. 28: John Edward Saché, Bara Chattar Manzil from the River Gomti, with the Chota Chattar Manzil and Darshan Bilas beyond, photographer's ref 193, albumen print, c. 1867, 187 x 280 mm.

Fig. 29: John Edward Saché, Bara Chattar Manzil from the River Gomti, photographer's ref. 200, albumen print, c. 1867, 234 x 286 mm.

Fig. 30: Shepherd & Robertson, Bara Chattar Manzil and Farhat Bakhsh, south side, photographer's ref. 335, albumen print, c. 1862, 252 x 361 mm.

Fig. 32: Felice Beato, The courtyards of the Qaisarbagh from the Roshan-ud-daula Kothi, six albumen prints, 1858, 256 x 1785 mm.

Fig. 33: John Edward Saché, The Safaid Barahdari and the 'Pigeon House' (on the far right) in the Jilau Khana, Qaisarbagh, photographer's ref. 158, albumen print, c. 1867, 214 x 274 mm.

Fig. 34: Unknown photographer, The Lanka in the Jilau Khana, Qaisarbagh, albumen print, 1860s, 183 x 245 mm.

Fig. 35: Shepherd & Robertson, The Great Vine and the Lanka, Qaisarbagh, photographer's ref. 329, albumen print, c. 1862, 240 x 397 mm.

Fig. 36: John Edward Saché, The Lanka, Qaisarbagh, photographer's ref. 164, albumen print, c. 1867, 223 x 285 mm.

Fig. 37: Frith's Series, The Lanka, Qaisarbagh, photographer's ref. 3045, albumen print, mid-1870s, 160 x 207 mm.

Fig. 38: John Edward Saché, Chaulakhi Gateway leading out of the Jilau Khana, Qaisarbagh, albumen print, c. 1867, 217 x 282 mm.

Fig. 39: Shepherd & Robertson, Chaulakhi Gateway into the Jilau Khana, Qaisarbagh, photographer's ref. 327, albumen print, c. 1862, 255 x 380 mm.

Fig. 40: Samuel Bourne, Jal Pari (the Mermaid Gateway), Qaisarbagh, photographer's ref. 1041, albumen print, December 1864–early 1865, 235 x 292 mm.

Fig. 41: Felice Beato, Jal Pari (the Mermaid Gateway) and spiral staircases, Qaisarbagh, albumen print, 1858, 264 x 305 mm.

Fig. 42: Samuel Bourne, Roshan-ud-daula Kothi, photographer's ref. 1046, albumen print, December 1864–early 1865, 106 x 194 mm.

Fig. 43: Frith's Series, Roshan-ud-daula Kothi, south side, photographer's ref. 343, albumen print, mid-1870s, 156 x 204 mm.

Fig. 44: Frith's Series, Roshan-ud-daula Kothi, north side, albumen print, 1870s, 227 x 284 mm.

Fig. 45: Samuel Bourne, The Jilau Khana, Qaisarbagh, with the tombs of Saadat Ali Khan and Begum Khurshid Zadi, photographer's ref. 1037, albumen print, December 1864–early 1865, 233 x 290 mm.

Fig. 46: Robert Tytler and Harriet Tytler, attrib., Tomb of Saadat Ali Khan, albumen print, c. 1858, 340 x 398 mm.

Fig. 47: Frith's Series, Tomb of Begum Khurshid Zadi, albumen print, 1870s, 208 x 160 mm.

Fig. 48: Felice Beato, The Bara Imambara and environs, eight albumen prints, 1858, 233 x 2375 mm.

Fig. 49: Shepherd & Robertson, Bara Imambara Gateway, photographer's ref. 345, albumen print, c. 1862, 268 x 365 mm.

Fig. 52: Unknown photographer, Rumi Darwaza, albumen print, 1890s, 214 x 271 mm.

Figs. 53 and 54: Unknown photographer, Rumi Darwaza and gateway of the Bara Imambara (left) with *jawab* (Facsimile Gateway) opposite, albumen print, late 1860s, 215 x 275 mm.

Fig. 55: The Phototype Company, Gateway leading into the third courtyard, Bara Imambara complex, postcard, late 1890s, 88 x 136 mm.

Fig. 56: Unknown photographer, Detail of the *jawab* (Facsimile Gateway), Bara Imambara complex, gelatin silver print, 1912–13, 105 x 81 mm.

Fig. 57: Samuel Bourne, The Bara Imambara complex showing the second courtyard, Imambara and Asafi Mosque, photographer's ref. 1052, albumen print, December 1864–early 1865, 240 x 292 mm.

Fig. 59: Unknown photographer, The Bara Imambara under restoration, albumen print, 1870s, 216 x 278 mm.

Fig. 65: Felice Beato, The south-west façade of the Bara Imambara, photographer's ref. L 46, albumen print, 1858, 249 x 295 mm.

Fig. 66: Unknown photographer, The rear, or south façade, of the Bara Imambara, albumen print, 1870s, 185 x 234 mm.

Fig. 67: Shepherd & Robertson, Asafi Mosque, west side, and Bara Imambara, south side, with the earth barricades from the Revolt of 1857, photographer's ref. 344, albumen print, c. 1862, 253 x 358 mm.

Fig. 68: G. W. Lawrie & Co., The rear, or south side, of the Bara Imambara, gelatin silver print, 1890s, 240 x 295 mm.

Fig. 69: Shepherd & Robertson, Asafi Mosque in the Bara Imambara complex, albumen print, c. 1862, 252 x 375 mm.

Fig. 70: Unknown photographer, Gateway leading from the third courtyard into the second courtyard, Bara Imambara, gelatin silver print, 1912–13, 80 x 105 mm.

Fig. 71: Felice Beato, Two-part panorama of the Husainabad Imambara, the Daulat Khana to the left, the Rumi Darwaza and Great Imambara to the right, albumen prints, 1858, 240 x 567 mm.

Fig. 72: John Edward Saché, Husainabad Bazaar Gateway, albumen print, c. 1867.

Fig. 73: Shepherd & Robertson, The Husainabad Imambara, Entrance Gateway seen from inside the complex, photographer's ref. 350, albumen print, c. 1862, 265 x 357 mm.

Fig. 74: Samuel Bourne, Tomb of Zinat Algiya and the Husainabad Mosque, photographer's ref. 1069, albumen print, December 1864–early 1865, 107 x 192 mm.

Fig. 75: Frith's Series, *Jawab* opposite the Tomb of Zinat Algiya at the Husainabad Imambara, photographer's ref. 3057, albumen print, late 1860s, 160 x 207 mm.

Fig. 76: John Edward Saché,
Tomb of Zinat Algiya, with the mosque
to the right, Husainabad Imambara,
photographer's ref. 188, albumen print,
c. 1867, 232 x 284 mm.

Fig. 77: Edmund David Lyon,
Jawab facing the Tomb of Zinat Algiya
at the Husainabad Imambara,
albumen print, c. 1862, 168 x 186 mm.

Fig. 78: Unknown photographer,
Husainabad Imambara and *jawab* facing
the Tomb of Zinat Algiya on the left,
postcard, late 1890s, 90 x 139 mm.

Fig. 79: John Edward Saché,
Husainabad Imambara, with the Tomb
of Zinat Algiya on the right,
photographer's ref. 185, albumen print,
c. 1867, 238 x 293 mm.

Fig. 80: Unknown photographer,
Husainabad Imambara, View across the *talao*,
albumen print, 1860s, 183 x 235 mm.

Fig. 81: Unknown photographer,
The Husainabad Imambara, showing
the calligraphy on the façade, albumen print,
late 1870s, 218 x 276 mm.

Fig. 82: Unknown photographer,
Husainabad Imambara, albumen print,
1870s, 183 x 235 mm.

Fig. 83: Unknown photographer,
The Karbala Kazmain, salt print,
c. 1856, 176 x 229 mm.

Fig. 84: The Phototype Company,
Imambara Shah Najaf (Najaf-i-Ashraf),
postcard, late 1890s, 89 x 136 mm.

Fig. 85: John Edward Saché,
The Husainabad *talao* and Bazaar Gateway,
with Sat Khande on the right and Jama Masjid
in the distance, photographer's ref. 191,
albumen print, c. 1867, 207 x 270 mm.

Fig. 86: G. W. Lawrie & Co., View across
the *talao* towards the Husainabad Bazaar
Gateway, with the Jama Masjid beyond,
gelatin silver print, 1890s, 206 x 271 mm.

Fig. 87: Unknown photographer,
Jama Masjid, postcard, c. 1912–13,
88 x 138 mm.

Fig. 88: Samuel Bourne, Dilkusha Kothi,
photographer's ref. 1149, albumen print,
December 1864–early 1865, 241 x 291 mm.

Fig. 90: Darogha Ubbas Alli, Bibiapur Kothi,
Plate 3 from *The Lucknow Album*, albumen
print, published 1874, 104 x 151 mm.

Fig. 93: John Edward Saché, Shops along
Hazratganj, including the photographer's
studio, photographer's ref. a.13, albumen print,
c. 1871, 197 x 312 mm.

Fig. 94: Samuel Bourne, Southern end
of Hazratganj, looking north-west,
photographer's ref. 1152, albumen print,
December 1864–early 1865, 188 x 302 mm.

Fig. 95: Darogha Ubbas Alli,
The offices of the 'Oudh and Rohilkund
Railway Company', Hazratganj,
Plate 9 from *The Lucknow Album*,
albumen print, published 1874, 104 x 151 mm.

Fig. 96: Darogha Ubbas Alli, Dilaram Kothi,
Plate 47 from *The Lucknow Album*,
albumen print, c. 1870, published 1874,
104 x 151 mm.

Fig. 97: Darogha Ubbas Alli, Hayat Bakhsh Kothi, also known as Banks' Bungalow, Plate 7 from *The Lucknow Album*, albumen print, c. 1870, published 1874, 104 x 151 mm.

Fig. 98: Darogha Ubbas Alli, Kankarwali Kothi, Plate 20 from *The Lucknow Album*, albumen print, published 1874, 104 x 151 mm.

Fig. 99: Unknown photographer, Nur Bakhsh Kothi, albumen print, c. 1865, 117 x 164 mm.

Fig. 100: Unknown photographer, Khurshid Manzil, albumen print, c. 1865, 56 x 94 mm.

Fig. 107: Darogha Ubbas Alli, Dilkusha Kothi, Plate 5 from *The Lucknow Album*, albumen print, 1860s, published 1874, 104 x 151 mm.

Fig. 108: John Edward Saché, Dilkusha Kothi, photographer's ref. 198 h, albumen print, c. 1867, 214 x 272 mm.

Fig. 109: Unknown photographer, Dilkusha Kothi, albumen print, 1880s, 102 x 148 mm.

Fig. 110: Unknown photographer, Dilkusha Kothi, garden façade, albumen print, 1870s, 185 x 236 mm.

Fig. 111: P. G. Fitzgerald, Alam Bagh, albumen print, February 1858, 168 x 238 mm.

Fig. 112: Felice Beato, Taronwali Kothi (the Observatory), albumen print, 1858, 237 x 301 mm.

Fig. 113: G. W. Lawrie & Co., Ruins of the Residency, gelatin silver print, 1890s, 205 x 280 mm.

Fig. 115: Unknown photographer, Baillie Guard Gate, British Residency, albumen print, 1870s, 237 x 291 mm.

Fig. 116: Unknown photographer, The Banqueting Hall in the Residency compound, albumen print, 1870s, 216 x 275 mm.

Fig. 117: Unknown photographer, Imambara Sharaf-un-Nissan and Masjid, adjacent to the Begum Kothi, in the Residency compound, albumen print, 1870s, 100 x 147 mm.

Fig. 118: John Edward Saché, Monument to 'Sir Henry Lawrence and Heroes', photographer's ref 187, albumen print, c. 1867, 285 x 225 mm.

Fig. 119: John Edward Saché, The spire of Christ Church seen from Wingfield Park, albumen print, c. 1867, 236 x 286 mm.

Fig. 120: Unknown photographer, Banqueting Hall seen from the Residency Tower, with the Chattar Manzil and Qaisarbagh beyond, albumen print, 1870s, 210 x 278 mm.

Fig. 121: Felice Beato, Steamboat shaped as a fish, and the nawab's pinnace *The Sultan of Oude* at the Bara Chattar Manzil, photographer's ref. L 29, albumen print, 1858, 247 x 302 mm.

Fig. 122: **Ahmad Ali Khan**, Pavilions in the River Gomti, bridging the Summer Palace/ Chattar Manzil and Dilaram Kothi, albumen print, c. 1856, 138 x 189 mm.

Fig. 123: **Mushkoor-ud-Dowlah or Asghar Jan**, Pavilion in the River Gomti, between the Summer Palace and Dilaram Kothi, albumen print, 1860s, 213 x 274 mm.

Fig. 124: **Felice Beato**, Bridge of boats over the River Gomti, the Chattar Manzil beyond, albumen print, 1858, 245 x 306 mm.

Fig. 125 **Felice Beato**, Bridge of boats over the River Gomti, La Martinière in the distance, albumen print, 1858, 237 x 303 mm.

Fig. 127: **Felice Beato**, The Iron Bridge, with Hindu temple on the left, photographer's ref. L42, albumen print, 1858, 227 x 303 mm.

Fig. 128: **Edmund David Lyon**, La Martinière, albumen print, c. 1862, 162 x 191 mm.

Fig. 130: **Unknown photographer**, 'Banks' Bungalow', formerly Claude Martin's arsenal, also known as Hayat Bakhsh Kothi, albumen print, c. 1856, 142 x 215 mm.

Fig. 132: **Unknown photographer**, The Tomb of Boulone Lize, with La Martinière in the background, albumen stereoscopic print (detail), March/April 1858, 66 x 69 mm.

Fig. 134: **Frith's Series**, La Martinière and the *lath*, albumen print, 1870s, 228 x 285 mm.

Fig. 135: Frith's Series,
La Martinière, albumen print,
mid-1870s, 158 x 210 mm.

Fig. 136: Frith's Series,
La Martinière and the *lath*,
albumen print, 1870s, 160 x 210 mm.

Fig. 137: Unknown photographer,
La Martinière, albumen print, c. 1880,
205 x 273 mm.

Fig. 141: Samuel Bourne,
La Martinière, garden side, albumen print,
December 1864–early 1865, 100 x 192 mm.

Fig. 142: Unknown photographer,
La Martinière and the *lath*, albumen print,
1870s, 188 x 240 mm.

Fig. 143: Unknown photographer,
La Martinière and the *lath*, view across the
Tank, albumen print, 1870s, 205 x 275 mm.

Back Endpaper: John Edward Saché,
La Martinière and the *lath*,
photographer's ref. 198d, albumen print,
c. 1867, 211 x 279 mm.

INDEX